T0192988

GOING TO GROUND

Caitlin Press Inc.
3375 Ponderosa Way
Qualicum Beach, BC V9K 2J8
www.caitlin-press.com

Text and cover design by Vici Johnstone
Edited by Jane Silcott
Printed in Canada

Caitlin Press Inc. acknowledges financial support from the Government of Canada and the Canada Council for the Arts, and the Province of British Columbia through the British Columbia Arts Council and the Book Publisher's Tax Credit.

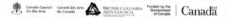

Library and Archives Canada Cataloguing in Publication
Going to ground : essays on aging, chronic pain and the healing power of nature
  / by Luanne Armstrong.

Armstrong, Luanne, 1949- author.
Canadiana 20210320885 | ISBN 9781773860756 (softcover)

LCGFT: Essays.
LCC PS8551.R7638 G65 2022 | DDC C814/.54—dc23

GOING TO GROUND

Essays on Aging, Chronic Pain and
the Healing Power of Nature

LUANNE ARMSTRONG

CAITLIN PRESS 2022

"The vision comes and goes, mostly goes, but I live for it, for the moment when the mountains open and a new light roars in spate through the crack, and the mountains slam."
—Annie Dillard

This book is dedicated to my grandkids and their future.

I acknowledge that I am working on the ancestral and unceded homelands of the Ktunaxa Nation and of the Sinixt People. In particular, I honour the Yakan Nu'kiiy People and I thank them for this privilege.

Contents

INTRODUCTION

My thinking and writing about land and the non-human world have been evolving since I was five and really looked at the world for the first time. I was feeding chickens and the field beside me glowed emerald green in the late afternoon sun, and I fell in love with beauty and being needed by chickens. Although I had no language for it, I knew what beauty was.

I have been asking myself the same question, really, since that moment: What does it mean to live somewhere? What does it mean to live somewhere and also have a relationship with the non-human (and human) inhabitants of that place, including the water, the rocks, the wind, the weather?

I learned to read and write at six and instantly decided to become a writer because even then I knew that language was my world. I also spent my growing years farming with my family and living intensely with animals, in the wild places around our farm, and inside, reading, always reading, especially books about animals where the animals were always the heroes and the humans weren't much good.

Now I am seventy-two, still on the same land; I have written two books about land and living in place, and I am still thinking more intensely than ever about where I live. In the time since the last book, I have had two car accidents and the resulting brain injury has made me very ill and somewhat disabled and in chronic pain for the last seven years. In a sense the accidents threw me into another country, another way of being—they threw me into disability and into age. Aging is a bigger identity crisis than being adolescent, but it is hardly talked about or written about. So, this book is about coming to terms with aging as well as making the long struggle to recover my sense of self, recover my ability to cook, clean, and shop, and more importantly, my ability to read, to write, to think deeply again. Chronic disease, chronic pain changes your sense of identity, changes the way you exist in the world, and yet some things are the same.

I garden, write, teach. I observe the world around me, both the human world and the non-human world. I was part of a very particular movement of people who deliberately tried to go "back to the land" in the late 1970s (well, I had never left), and I watched as that movement disintegrated. Now I am watching as one of my children becomes part of a new "young farmer" movement. But I am old. I try hard to not carp, and no one asks my advice.

I am also, of course, reading about and watching in the news the various scientists who are predicting with deep desperation and deepening pessimism the prospects of a world with increasing warming and disruptive climate change.

This new book is called *Going to Ground* because it is a series of essays about all these things: aging and living with pain; pessimism and hope; working with animals; observing the non-human world; the strange articulation of living somewhere between normalcy and apocalypse; the human inability to perceive the slow change of destruction and the same human easy ability to gobble away at the world without perceiving how much we change it as we do. I am so heartened by the new work and discoveries of the sentience, the intelligence, the communication, the cultures, of the non-human. This knowledge ultimately is what will turn our world back towards the light of care and understanding.

ALWAYS THERE

Rewilding

This spring I walked across the bottom field of my farm, crunching my way through the tall canary grass that had formed grey-green mats over the field and the baby fir trees, barely sprung from the wet ground and reaching for the light. Land everywhere records its history and then buries it. Buildings buckle and fall down; pavement cracks with fungi, and then grass and tall strong plants like thistles and burdocks appear, precursors to the forest that will one day grow there if the land is left alone.

I am watching the farm transform. Every day, I walk among ghosts: dead orchards, dead house, parts of machines. Old paths. Old ways. The old names we made as children. I will take them with me into the house of the dead.

I thread my way through towers of bright timothy, tansy, and burdock. The grass is high except for the places where the geese and elk have eaten their fill. But no one eats the tall grey grass going to seed. It should have been cut for hay, but my brother and I are now too old to do such work. My brother doesn't come to the farm anymore. He has turned away from the farm and from me, bitter at how much time and energy the farm and I demanded of him. He and my siblings grew up in a family where, if we got sick, my father said, "Go outside and work it off." I was ill and then my brother's wife as well. It was a hard time and the burden on him was heavy, too heavy.

So now there are no cows to eat the pasture down to its roots. There are no pigs joyfully rooting for mud. There should be hay piled in the shed. There should be a bright rainbow of chickens happily chasing grasshoppers.

But the tall grass has its own presence, its own multi-layered, multi-coloured, shape-shifting knowledge. Grass grows in order to be eaten, and it rarely dies except in severe droughts. All over the planet, in a process still not clearly understood by science, grass turns light into energy which becomes food for grazing animals. The tall gold-green-orange grass in my fields gulps down light. It mats the ground in the fall and makes shelter for mice and voles and earthworms and snakes. But grass is the precursor to forest and every spring, new green pine and Douglas fir shoots poke their noses through. Left undisturbed, this field in fifty years would be a huge forest.

How to feel about this?

Once the farm was all urgency and hurry; farm jobs don't wait. This sense of hurry-hurry has stayed with me all my life, through everything I've done, but now I don't hurry because I can't. So I watch and wait.

On the farm, we hurried to harvest it all when it was time: myriad fruits and vegetables, towers of food brought in and left to my hurrying mother to transform into food for winter.

The hay was cut according to the sun and the CBC weather reports; the sun had to stay for at least a week or longer so the hay would dry properly. Rain was sometimes a disaster, sometimes a salvation. Rain split and rotted the cherries, ruined the hay and took all the food value out of it. But rain was necessary for spring, for new grass, for the garden, for everything else. If rain didn't come, there was an elaborate system of sprinklers all over that ensured the farm's continuity as a green oasis The sprinklers had to be moved every day, usually by me.

I don't know how to feel about this either. I loved farming. I loved the days when the farm bustled with activity. The back door of the house slammed many times a day with people in and out, working, eating, talking and talking, the radio always on. I loved being part of it, being strong, never tired.

Often, on my last walk at night, I pass the other house, the old house in which we all grew up, empty now. When I die, it will have no one left who believed in its life. The many people who once crowded there are far away or gone altogether, and there's no life there now except in the summer when bats move in and explode out the broken windows at dusk.

So many things did live there once. The old house was built by Pierre Longueval, the original homesteader. He cut down huge cedar trees, milled the lumber, built the house room by room. But it was already old when we moved in, insulated with layers of newspaper and bits of sawdust.

All her married life, my mother wanted a new house. She hated the old gloomy house beside the highway because it was in a hollow beside the road and had no view and was always cold and damp. She longed for a place where she could cook and do dishes and still see the lake and the mountains because the older she got, the more rarely she went outside. She wanted to be able to entertain, although having people for tea or dinner made her nervous and afraid of their judgement. She wanted a new stove and new pots and pans. She wanted to be warm. All my life, my mother was always cold. Winter and summer, our father stoked the stoves all day for her sake.

But even though she didn't like it, when we were growing up, the old house rang with energy, shone with noise and colour—our parents, us, and the animals—cats and kittens, dogs, bats, and mice. The farm was like a model of all farms through time, with many people in and out the door, serious about working; the man coming in the house at evening from doing chores, the woman's voice calling, the scents of roast beef and stewed chicken. At night, our children's hearts beat contentedly under the covers, the cold outside caught and held by the thin board walls.

There were places all around the house with names and stories, so the house had a map of its own. For us children, every place on the farm was marked by secret names, known only by us.

The farm is only a momentary clear-cut in the long vision of time. It carries the footprints of the present and the past, the men who sweated and killed things to make their place here. It holds the names of my father, his father before him, and Pierre Longueval.

Once the majestic sternwheelers rolled along the lake-shore; then a railroad crawled north, hammered down by hand, each railway spike, each tie, each rail, along the west shore of the lake. The mule track beside Pierre's house became a highway.

But this land also ate my father up, called him to work, stooped his shoulders and filled him with rage. This land would neither help him nor let him go.

And then, finally, my father's great gift to my mother— on top of the work on the farm and the work off the farm—he began building her a new house. My grandfather had died and left them enough money so that my father could buy a back-hoe and build septic tanks and drain fields for other people. He began blowing up the basement for the new house when I was young; he drilled the holes with an ancient gas-powered drill, stuffed them with dynamite and stumping powder, and blew rocks all over the place. Then he cut down the trees to build a log house, peeled them and stacked them to dry.

Every once in a while, he would get enough time to put up another row of logs. He cut the seams out with a chainsaw, then stacked the logs with the backhoe.

Then my father bought a small portable sawmill, cut down some more trees, and began making lumber. We all sort of forgot about the house, but slowly it grew, log by log, board by board, my father working until late with a trouble light, a hammer, a fistful of nails. When he got the concrete poured into the hole in the rocks for a basement, he got a planer, a radial arm saw, and parked them in the basement. Inside the concrete and logs.

He made lumber out of "blue pine," pine trees that had been killed by pine beetles so the boards had dark grey-blue streaks in them.

My parents decided to buy everything new: all new appliances, a new TV, new chairs, a new bed. I moved home from teaching college in 1989, and my mother picked up her favourite saucepan, walked across the yard, and moved into her new house, high on a rocky promontory, looking over the lake. I think it was one of the happiest days of her life.

Every day now I walk between the house my father built and the water and see clouds spilling over the cold blue of the Selkirks, streaming and spitting snow. Kootenay Lake steams and huffs into the wind, and I turn my face to whatever dream the mountains might give me. The windows of the house my father built are haloed against the dark, light rushing out.

How do I feel about this?

I grew up feral. That is where my affinities still lie: for the bear beyond the yard light; the deer stepping lightly, ears fanned and wide; for the coyote in the field, teaching her pups to hunt mice; for the cougar on the hill; for me, the self who found the wild places and went there. When I was a child, I spent more of my time with animals than with people. But I was also a good farmer. I didn't see the contradiction.

I did my chores after school, I fed the chickens, I collected the eggs, I fed the cows their hay, and then I went to the woods. Stepping into the forest was always a relief, a sense of being safe, protected and known. I was never afraid. I went as far as I could in the small time between chores and supper. In summers I went to the lake, swam, fished, or crouched on the rocks as dusk came, as the evening wind slid down the hill and smacked the lake surface into silver, and then I could walk home in the dark shadows that pooled under the cedar trees. Being outside in the windy wild dusk is still my favourite thing.

But I am a farmer who can't farm anymore and during summers now, the farm crouches, beaten under by the noise of industrialized recreation. All around me there are Sea-Doos, jet boats, motorcycles without mufflers. Retired people chainsaw, mow and Roundup their small yards into subservience, not realizing that if they relax for one moment it will all spring back again. What are they achieving, these strange people, in making everything around them into a lawn that no one walks on, no one eats from, where trees can only be so tall, and must be whacked into size? I cheer for every small green twig shooting up from a crack in the rocks to defy them. For the fairy ring mycelium that persists in dancing circles into their lawns. For the horsetail in the creek which gleefully springs back to life no matter how much it is weed whacked or forced to drink Roundup. For the meltwater that gullies their road in the spring.

What do they see now when they see me walk the wild fields of what was once a farm, sprung now to wild grass and the wave of new pines, slowly making a forest? The grass hasn't been mowed for the last three years. In late summer, it is taller than I am.

Do they see me as a crazy person wandering these lost fields, through the dead orchard, past the broken house, into my own house, my father's house, also untended, and which stays together only because it cares for me? Outside, the one fir seedling that sprouted among the rocks in the summer of my father's dying, sixteen years ago, is now over twenty feet tall. I water it, I talk to it, I wish it well. I won't be able to stay here to watch it grow.

How do I feel about this?

My children think I am preoccupied by death. Instead, I am preoccupied by the multiple complexities of aging, a fascinating new territory that I won't be able to find my way out of. I have been so many people, worn so many labels, and now this one, full of small shocks, some more bewildering than others. Every day I ask, how do I feel about this? How can I feel about this? More and more I relax into my own rewilding, not as an old woman, but as a woman with an odd new freedom. Not much is expected of me; my children want me to be safe, and I want the opposite: to go wild again, to be left alone.

People use many voices with those they perceive as old; nurse voices: concerned, fake concerned, reasonable, lecturing, with a hint of razor blade and punishment just past the lecture. Are you depressed? Are you taking your pills properly? Are you resting enough? Why can't you just take it easy? Just relax? Stay safe. Be careful. Don't slip. Drive carefully. All said to me by faraway, worried children.

None of these things have anything to do with me, with the person I am, the person I was, the wild girl, the old woman, one and the same. I am now rewilding amid the fallen-over golden grass. I am the woman at the lakeshore in the evening, waiting for the shadows to slide over the blue Selkirks, then walking home, greeting the bright-red-barked giant pines, the dancing cedars.

I walk by the falling grapes, the flashing gold pears, the bear-wounded apple trees, unable to harvest them, process them, lay them all away for winter, for the long nights and the painful mornings. How do I feel about this? How will I know until I can look back? How can I look back when there is nowhere else to go? How should I feel about this? How can I feel about this?

This is the hardest thing, to walk past the plum tree shivering with red-gold fruit. Once when I was very young, I sat under a plum tree and ate/drank so many plums there was simply no room left in my belly for one more. As time went on, I would even dress up for this, wear a purple t-shirt, make a ritual of it, or I would walk to the peach tree when the first peach dropped, a sign the peaches were ready to pick, and pick the first, ripest, softest peach, and savour it. I would celebrate my relationship with this tree that I had planted, then pruned, watered, and picked, every year—that first peach a sacrament. It was deeply erotic in the best way, not sexual but loving, loving the trees that gave me so much beauty and abundance.

So much of my life has been built around the sacrament of growing food, picking it, sharing it with people, all kinds of people. Having to slowly let go of that is a grief I carry. Perhaps it's better now that the bears, the deer, the ravens, the raccoons, the birds, have access to it all. They need the food as well. They are welcome now.

But it is still a huge struggle for me, to go against years of training, to call the dogs away, bring them in the house at night, and let the bears have the apples. When I was a child, my father guarded and protected his crops with a gun, with traps, with curse words. The bears and ravens were his particular enemies because our cash crops were cherries, apples, pears, and plums. It was a constant battle in the fall to keep the bears out of the trees.

During the fall months, bears need to put on weight to prepare for winter and hibernation. This process is called hyperphagia. Bears are normally polite animals with a deep respect for boundaries but when they are driven to eat and their neighbour has food dripping off his trees, it's pretty hard to discourage them.

Perhaps it's better now to walk by with the black dog and the white cat on our way to see what there is to see. I walk, I watch, I wait. However much I try to shake off my farming self, it is still there, growling back at the bears.

WALKING WITH CARAIGH

The first time I rode him, I sat still, trying to get a sense of this new horse before asking him to move. I am a semi-disabled rider with rheumatoid arthritis, so I am always cautious with a new horse. Then I asked him to move forward. My sister was riding beside me. Not watching me but noticing everything, as she does. We rode out over the winter field, the grass tall and yellow, the wind coming in off the grey lake, shooting bits of ice at us, biting our skin through our clothes.

As the horse moved, a sense of strength and calm came up through my body. We went on along by the lake, up through the forest and back over the field to the barn. I slid off, took off the bridle and saddle and turned him loose. Instead of running off to be with the other horses, as most horses would do, he turned, shoved his nose into my chest, and heaved a big sigh.

My sister laughed. "Hey," she said. "He's your horse. He's picked you to be his person."

I didn't know about that yet, but I said to my sister, "Then let's change his name." He had come to the farm with the name Chris, a dull name for an ugly horse.

We had both just read an unapologetically romantic book about the first Scottish king, whose horse's name was Caraigh, which apparently means rock in Gaelic. So we gave him an unapologetically romantic name. A romantic name for this big red horse who tended to trip over his own legs and who often stood in the corner of the pasture away from the other horses, his too-big head dangling off his thin neck, a horse no one wanted and no one had ever really loved. My sister had picked him out of a group of horses that had been turned out on a big piece of land to graze. They were stallions with bands of mares and they kept Caraigh away from food and water. He was a horse with a broken heart and he needed care, better food, and someone who loved him.

I have always loved horses and never known why. Horses came into my life just as my family and I moved to our farm, just as I grew into being a wild girl with a wild country all around me. I was turning six. The neighbour girls came through our yard on horseback, chasing a herd of skinny cows. My dad yelled something about "broomtails." Where we lived on Kootenay Lake was then "open range," which meant that farmers could let their livestock run loose and people had to fence them out.

The next day, I walked the mile of gravel road in my bare feet to find those horses. Horses and I have hung out together ever since.

My sister has also been riding since she was a kid. But my sister is a magic horse whisperer woman. She's a farrier and a horse trainer. Not that she really has magic powers. But she sees stuff. She has been hanging out with horses so long that she sees right through them to the horse they could be. Even when they are running away or trying to kick her.

When she first saw Caraigh, he had been mostly ignored by everyone. No one wanted to buy him because he has what is called, unkindly, but accurately, a jughead, meaning his head looks too big, hanging off the skinny rest of his neck and body. But my sister knew he could be my horse when she brought him to me. I have a bad neck too. Mine is full of kinks and knots and gives me killer headaches. And I have a broken heart as well; mine only beats because a pacemaker forces it.

Caraigh and I now work together at the Therapeutic Riding Centre where he works as a therapy horse. I also get to take riding lessons on him. Part of what we are doing is learning to communicate together. He gets impatient with my slowness to understand. The last time he had a sore back, he started nipping me, not hard, but it was a bit scary, until I finally figured it out and got him some massage.

Because I have been around horses all my life, other people have always told me how to be around them. "Show that broomtail who's boss," said my dad when I was a little kid and riding my first horse, an unbroken, untrained mare who was smarter than me about most things.

Use this thing, people would say, about the whips, reins, and harsh bits to make horses do this or that. Never just *listen, walk, pay attention*. When I listen to my body and the horse's body, we breathe together, walk within this bubble, this forcefield of really paying attention and connecting our bodies on some level I don't understand, but know how to work with.

I try to work with Caraigh with the same kind of mindfulness that I would give to meditation or a martial art. Riding uses the same stances and similar energy to martial art. Simply being on a horse exercises all the joints and muscles in the human body. It strengthens the inner core. The rider is constantly tuned to her own body and the horse's body. After I ride, my concentration is sharper. I drive better. I think better.

On good riding days, my horse and I become a dyad, almost one body. Horses are attuned to body movement; Caraigh connects to my body movements and we move within this connection. Once when I was just leading him around the riding ring, someone called my name and I raised my head and turned my shoulders to look at her, and Caraigh tried to turn, as my shoulders signalled to him, and he bumped into me.

Stupid human. I apologized as best I could.

I also teach writing. I have done this for a long time now. I have taught in many places to a whole variety of people. I tell people that the best place to start writing is from a place of unknowing, confusion even. That feeling ignorant and stupid is part of writing. My students are earnest, hard-working, attentive people. They mistrust everything I tell them. But I have published books and they haven't, so they listen. I make them write.

But often they believe that if I can only tell them the right magic trick, writing will happen the way writing happens in movies, where an impassioned writer, struck by inspiration, stays up all night, crumples page after page, but somehow emerges into the grey morning light with a pile of brilliant words that are immediately swept up by a publisher. Fame and fortune follow.

Of course, nothing works that way, least of all writing— or riding.

Riding takes years of practice and developing the right movements and muscles and seat bones and awareness of where the horse's feet are and which muscles he is using. When someone first gets on a horse to learn to ride, the teacher says indecipherable things like *move with the horse, keep your hands still, head up, look where you are going.* Eventually, riding starts to make sense. You have to let the horse's body move your body, which seems impossible until you relax and understand that you won't fall off.

Writing is also not only years of practice but also a kind of surrendering to not knowing where the story is going or what the ending is. Very occasionally, I think I actually know something about both writing and riding.

But none of that matters when I am actually writing or riding. My riding teacher can ask me the theory of riding a twenty-metre circle and I can recite it: inside leg on, outside leg back, open the inside rein, balance with the outside rein. Sometimes I make a mess of it. Not always though. Sometimes Caraigh and I connect and ride a perfect circle and when I get off, he shoves his head into my chest and I tell him what a brilliant, beautiful horse he is.

Every time I start a new story, all the writing I've done and all the theory I've read won't save me. Can't save me. Any piece of writing can fail. All knowledge does is improve the odds that this time, I might succeed.

Competitive riding gets more difficult as I get better at it. The changes I need to make in my body and the signals I send to my horse get finer and smaller.

Writing is much the same. I do a lot of editing as well as writing and in the final stages of editing, the changes to a text get smaller and smaller but these changes have a big impact.

When I was young, I learned to ride, as many farm kids did, by having horses around. I stuck on my horse until I found out what worked and because I was young and athletic and had no fear, I could ride anywhere. Learning to ride well has been incredibly satisfying.

Writing for me was much the same. I wrote and I studied and I wrote some more. I still read about writing. There is always more to know.

On the other hand, I have been around horses all my life and some days I think I understand nothing. Horses are amazing, beautiful, responsive animals. I don't understand their humble attention to me and my demands. I don't understand why horses have acceded to domestication and more than their share of abuse through their history. There are no particular benefits to horses in being domesticated. Horses naturally live wild; domestic horses go wild with ease. Horse herd behaviour doesn't change when they are domesticated. Horses aren't particularly kind to each other, but they are often kind and caring with their riders.

Walking with Caraigh is like walking through sifted layers of history, through a fog of trying to understand, a misty romantic murmur of human beings and horses, of wildness and gentleness and humility and two bodies, attuned, turning in unison.

Somewhere, somehow, my body knows more than I do. When I forget to be in control, when I forget everything I know, I can ride a circle correctly, in rhythm with my horse, feet under me, hands where they should be, shoulders back, head up, as my riding teacher reminds me as often as I need it.

And sometimes, when I forget everything and I don't know what I am doing, I can write a good story. My body breathes along with the story, ideas show up, but I have no idea what I am doing or what I am writing or what the ending is. I pilgrimage endlessly and often, and if I am really lucky, I know nothing about where I am going. Or how to get there. Or what I might do if I ever arrive.

But at least I have figured out that the purpose of riding is joy. There are moments when Caraigh and I achieve what can only be called harmony. When our purposes coincide, when his stride smooths out, when I sit properly, when the circle is actually round, when his body and my body knit together, we achieve something. When I get off, he pushes his head into my chest and we stand together breathing. What have we done? Achieved something unknowable. The moment passes. He goes to eat grass and I go home and dream about riding. What does Caraigh dream? I will never know. So much I don't know. Less and less as time passes. Except how to sit up straight, push my heels down, look where I am going, relax, and ride squarely and gently into a circle.

Looking at Animals

My horse notices everything: the light flashing on a bird's wing or a deer's ear twitching. Sometimes he jumps at things I don't see at all. His ears flick and move constantly. On foot, beside him, I am in his field of view, just one of the many things he sees and considers. He doesn't look at me when I move, unless I do something strange or unexpected or suspicious, or completely weird in his terms, then he startles. He rarely focuses his gaze specifically on me. Instead, his look is wide, calm, peaceful, but alert. What interests him most, of course, is other horses. If one of those is on the way, perhaps from a pen, perhaps from a horse trailer, he knows immediately, his ears go forward, and his head goes up.

When we have a lesson with a particular trainer, he waits for the horse he had previously been pastured with to show up. He knows that this horse had been there the previous lessons with this trainer. He keeps one ear cocked towards the fence, one eye over there, noticing. And when this horse comes, he does nothing, but his ears relax. He can stop watching. Horses are demonstrative with each other, and they forget nothing. But when they are being ridden, they aren't allowed to socialize, one of the many small cruelties humans practise without noticing.

Looking at animals means noticing how and why they are looking back. This is hard to do. They don't make eye contact in the same way that people do with other people. They often don't make eye contact at all. They don't seem to look back at us. Except of course, they do. They see us and beyond us. They see so much of what is going on and far more than we see or sense, or smell or hear. They see us within an animal time that is probably much more present than our human present. Different, at least. They don't just see us, they hear and smell and touch us as well. When my dog comes back from circling out, she always touches my hand with her nose. Yes, it is really me.

All my life, I have been trying to look back at animals, to catch their eye, to see them, and it is a hard trick. For years I have been trying to notice what my horse sees, so I watch his ears and his eyes. But of course he sees so much that I don't catch, and he mostly looks past me. I am just not that interesting. He sees past me into the orchards or the forest beside the riding ring. Every time we go riding, I have to justify to myself what I am doing: "training" him, riding in circles, forcing him to do what I want.

As I age, I think more often that I shouldn't do this anymore. It seems a bit silly now to be ambitious and competitive although I have spent my life being that. But why force my horse into it?

Why make him do anything at all?

When I was young, I took my connection with animals for granted. I fed them, looked after them, played with them, helped my dad slaughter them. And I have spent a lot of time on both studying animals and reading what people think about them. My perspectives have changed and are still changing.

But in my elder age, I am very conscious that I have walked through this world as a kind of slave-owner. I am a farmer and I have kept animals. There is nothing romantic about farming. It's a system for producing food that involves a lot of dirt and shit and often blood. It can be done well. Animals can be treated with respect. When I raised pigs or chickens, they ran around in a pen, but in the sun. They got petted, talked to, and then eaten. Ethically, that is a very conflicted position and I know that now, and it remains unresolved within me and within the greater world.

Ever since—for no reason we really understand—some animals became domesticated, about ten thousand years ago, humans have seemed to take it as their right to stare, to hunt, to name, to see, to look, to watch, to know, to label, and all too often, to assume they know far more about the non-human than they really know.

Bird watchers, whale watchers, bear watchers, and eco-tourists all relentlessly look, stare, take for granted their right to stare and record the results.

In Indigenous stories of animals, the animals are the teachers: they talk, play jokes on humans, or have sex with them.

John Berger points out that one result of looking is, ultimately, the complete marginalization of animals, captured and held in zoos where they become mere decoration, unable to respond or look back. He writes, "However you look at these animals, even if the animal is up against the bars, less than a foot from you, looking outward in the public direction, you are looking at something that has been rendered absolutely marginal."

I am aware that I walk through this world, both the domesticated world and the wild world as a top animal, as a predator, and therefore terrifying and something to be looked at by the non-human beings in this world in a particular way. There's not much I can do about it except stop staring, try to modify my body language, turn my hips away, to say, "I'm not hunting, I'm not going to kill you."

Since I was very young, animals have been in my life. Some have been companions, friends and only lately have I realized how much they were and are my teachers. I had no one to teach me about animals and how to be around them, except my father who was a farmer and a pioneer and understood animals from that point of view, which meant domination and eventually death.

I learned mostly from interaction and observation. When I was very young, I was around animals more than with people, especially in the summer, when there was no school. Mostly this was with the domestic animals on the farm; my farm chores usually involved feeding the cows and chickens, caring for baby chicks in the spring, gathering the eggs from the big chickens in the afternoons after school, and whatever else needed doing.

I was also good at fishing and I loved to be alone in the woods. I spent hours alone at the lake or on the mountain, usually, although not always, with a dog, not my dog, but the farm dog, whichever dog that was. We didn't have pet dogs.

I read all the animal books I could, novels mostly, and these were somewhat useful although usually sentimental and so badly written that even I got bored and sped through them. But some were wonderful and a few, like *The Yearling*, reflected the multiple contradictory dilemmas of my life back to me. But I didn't know that then. I only knew it was a wonderful book that I read over and over.

And then, after a lot of nagging, sulking and whining when I was eight, my dad bought me a totally unsuitable, untrained and unbroken horse, and I learned to ride. Not without some danger.

I started riding with the neighbours when we first moved to the farm. There were two girls who chased their varying herd of cows and horses down the gravel highway to graze and then rounded them up again at night. But they moved away and I was left with a scared, shy, unbroken three-year-old mare. I did the right thing without knowing what to do. She was lonely and I followed her around with apples and bits of grain stolen from the chickens. Eventually, she let me put a halter on her and even ride her. Horses ran through my dreams for all time after that.

But I was cruel to her out of ignorance. I had no idea about training, and so I thought she was "stubborn" and "lazy" (which is what people told me), and I often hit her with a stick or a braided leather quirt. I yanked on the reins to go anywhere. I rode bareback everywhere and in retrospect, I realize she took great care of me.

Once my father left me to ride her home the five miles along the highway from the summer pasture where she had been left with the cows. She hadn't seen me or any people for five months.

It was December, snowing and dark. I was eight years old. I rode with a halter and rope and when my hands got too cold to hold the rope, I simply lay forward on her neck, put my frozen hands under her thick, matted mane, and let her take me home.

The history of humanity is inextricably bound up with entanglement with animals and cruelty to animals. Yes, it is entirely probable that at various points in human history, humans were mainly vegetarian but there is also no question that humans are the most amazing food opportunists on the planet and will eat almost anything, including almost any form of animal flesh. And we are predators. And being a predator is innately cruel because it involves death.

Once we learned to domesticate animals and breed them to fit human needs, humans were much more able to move, to fight wars, and to have a ready supply of milk and meat.

Humans are omnivores but also predators. It is this ability to devour anything that has enabled people to move, to live and to survive, all over the world from the arctic to the desert, in every kind of ecosystem, and along the way, to domesticate and continue to eat animals, to use animals for farm work, and to develop a system that was in place for thousands of years, very similar to the one I grew up in, where everything on a farm helped to sustain everything else on the farm, and all of it was sustained by the physical labour of the farmers, which often included multiple people, children, and workers of various ages in varying relationships to the land.

It was a reasonably good working system which was almost completely overturned and destroyed by the industrialization of agriculture. So too, the relationships with domesticated animals were completely revised into an industrial model that now treats animals as products and their lives as insignificant.

There is no question that cruelty to animals has always been part of farming, but in my childhood, on our farm at least, there was also a rough sense of equality. Small farming was and is far from perfect, but for the farmers, there was some sense of partnership and engagement with the animals they used. Not all farmers care well for their animals, but it was usually in their best interests to do so.

Not only were animals entangled with my life as a child, but stories of animals ran through all my family's lives and dominated the dinner table. Animals were real characters to us, with vivid personalities about which endless epic anecdotes circled, including my father's battles with Tiny, the Jersey milk cow, when Tiny would take it in her head to run the seven miles south to find the neighbour's bull; my adventures with Lady, the horse, who could get out of any pen, who stopped the Greyhound bus by going to sleep on the highway, who destroyed a line of my mother's freshly washed sheets, and so on. Plus the endless dogs and cats who came and went in our lives, fiercely loved and easily lost. We learned very young not to weep over pet calves or pigs but to eat them instead, the process of butchering always fascinating, because my father made it so, the transition from live pet to dead meat in an instant. There was no time or room or space to sentimentalize about animals. We raised them, fed them, petted them, babied them—whether we loved them or not is impossible to say—and in the end, we ate them. I didn't think too much about it as a child, because I accepted then, and still accept with some pride, the self-sufficiency and toughness that enables someone to be a small farmer. And my father told me that it was what we must do.

I watched a YouTube film (not *Into the Wild*) about a man determined to spend time alone in the wilderness, to survive on his own. He went to Yukon, camped by a lake, lived there alone. He didn't bring enough food, thinking he could catch fish and other game, which to a limited extent, he did. He filmed himself, weeping into the camera, as he slowly broke down, afraid, blubbering, scared of bears, scared of the silence, mostly, terrified of the utter indifference of the land around him to his fate.

A dog would have made all the difference. A dog would have been company, would have warned him about bears, would have nestled beside him at night, licked his face, kept him from going crazy.

In another similar film series, a Norwegian man travels across Canada with a team of dogs. He hunts, fishes, falls in the river, films himself, not crying, but coping, dealing with the elements, at home because he is skilled and not alone and knows where he is and has dogs to protect him and to care for. He pays no attention to the indifference of the wilderness because he is equally indifferent to it, focused as he is on the survival of himself and his dogs. His dogs are the key to his survival; they pull his sleigh, help him hunt, keep him company, give him something to focus on. The two videos are completely different; one is desolate, and one is resolute.

It's interesting to watch children, very small children, and consider how they see animals. My grandson Louis, when he was about two, met a dog for the first time. He was enchanted with the dog. He asked the dog, "Do you want to play?"

The dog ignored him and went around the room, sniffed the furniture, and looked for food. His owner put a bowl of water on the floor and the dog had a drink. Louis found this equally enchanting and got down on the floor and lapped water with his tongue. He began to follow the dog around the room on his hands and knees, imitating his behaviour and still trying to play. The dog was somewhat irritated by this non-dog dog. In fact, Louis made the poor dog very nervous. Eventually, the big humans stepped in and separated the two. The interaction had not worked and the small human imitating a dog seemed to actually terrify the dog.

People do try all kinds of "natural" ways to connect with animals, but I think the best thing to do is to be a human being with as few assumptions as possible. People carry around all kinds of assumptions about animals. Being with animals when you have innate ingrained but untrue ideas about them is difficult.

People who come to my farm to camp or play on the beach find the thought that there might be a cougar some-where in the mountains near them frightening. I always tell my visitors we don't have cougars. Or bears. Or skunks. Or snakes. The fact that these animals are nearly always around and people just don't see them and aren't aware of them is not something such people find comforting if I point this out.

Nor is the fact that the countryside is full of bugs easy for them to deal with. I live in a log house. Putting up a log house is the equivalent of calling out "lunch" to all sorts of critters. I have bats in the roof and ants in the sill logs. Not that long ago, I was sitting on my deck with my grandson's new girlfriend from the city. She was struggling desperately to be nice and show her appreciation of all this nature but the bugs—flies, wasps, ants, and mosquitoes—did her in; she fled inside the house, which wasn't all that much of a shelter.

Ants come in every year, even though I tell them I will kill them, and do. In the winter, cedar bugs wander across my keyboard and I let them. They are blind but responsive to light and warmth. They wave their ridiculous antennae at me. I pick them up by their little noses and put them outside.

I have not the faintest idea about causation in any of this. It is all coincidence. I talk to animals and attempt to look them in the eye. What I don't do is believe in the results. I have no faith in what I am doing but I do it anyway. Just in case.

The internet is full of ultra-sentimentalized animal vid-eos. Cat videos are a running joke. But a lot of these videos fo-cus on animals being unnatural, behaving unlike themselves. Dogs and deer being friends, or a cat raising baby ducks, or a tiger nursing a baby baboon.

Or there are videos where wild animals hug and caress people or respond to people's psychic abilities. There are almost no popular videos about the reality of wild animal lives, or even domestic animal lives unless one searches them out as research videos. The ones that go viral on the internet always appeal to people's deepest, weirdest, and most sentimental and bizarre notions of how animals behave. The idea that animals are somehow like us or can be made to behave like furry humans runs deep. The whole notion of pet animals, once it is examined, takes on a peculiar shadow—and yet I myself have them. I do my best to not treat them as pets. They do their best to cajole, to beg, to earnestly turn me into a pet owner. But I am not and never will be a dog or cat "mom."

Between us, distorting the relationship, lies the power of food. I have the food. They hang out on the edge of my can opener. They are animals in their own kind of zoo, where I look at them and they look at the can of food in my hand. They are perfectly free to come and go and completely chained to me by the can opener as I am chained to them by their need and my training as a farmer, where you always feed your animals first.

Do I like their company? Yes, of course. Do I have a need for them? Yes, I need the cats to kill mice and the dogs to chase deer and cougars and bears away from the farm. It is an almost even trade. Do we love each other? I have no idea. The power of that can opener distorts our relationship. But we like each other, no question, we enjoy each other, we do things together, we have expectations of each other.

When she is anxious, my dog sticks her head between my knees and breathes and breathes and then runs away, tail waving like a white plume—happy—I am tempted to say, but here, language becomes a big problem. Whether any animals have feelings, as humans name emotions, is unknown. But they undoubtedly feel things deeply.

The problem is neither knowledge nor looking; the problem is naming.

Looking is, in fact, easy and doable. Understanding what I see is so intensely layered that it surprises me every day. For example, in the fall at the farm, it is always a struggle with the bears. They are very hungry and they want my apples and plums. I have far more than I can use and I am too crippled now to take care of these trees, to prune them in the spring and pick the fruit in the fall. For most of my life, I have called this jokingly, the bear wars. I would go out at night with my big dogs to chase off the bears. But this year I stopped.

The bears are especially hungry this year. It was too hot. The berries didn't ripen, instead they dried and fell off the bushes. The bears need food.

In part, I keep the dogs to chase bears, which keeps the bears safe. My neighbours' solution for a problem bear is to call the conservation officer and have the bear trapped and killed. I want the bears to be wary so they can be safe from my neighbours. Bears are normally polite, but in the fall they are desperately driven to eat.

But one night, I'd had enough. I put the dogs in the house, went outside and said, "Okay bears, it is all yours. Eat what you need and then go away."

All people should, I believe, look and see this world as much as possible. But we rarely have the language to name what we see. The media always names animals in clichés. Wild animals are invariably snarling, stalking, lying in wait, running amok; no matter how harmless they might actually be, they are named as a threat. Wild animals in space that humans have claimed for themselves are also seen as a threat.

We are in this world, as are animals and we share it on some kind of basis. But understanding and naming what you are seeing is a blockade of difficulty, of unknowability. Language stands in the way and fails. Animals clearly express contentment or fear or many other emotions. But we have no names for this. Scientists now cautiously name animals as sentient. It's hard to know exactly what this means. Animals are thinking, knowing, seeing, understanding, and figuring things out. How far does such sentience continue? What do they know of us, besides that we are a threat?

I have tried to imagine myself into my dogs' various lives but I am met immediately with a series of blocks. For one thing, it is hard enough to imagine myself into the mind and heart and emotions and actions of another human, even though, as a writer, I do it all the time.

But a dog lives in a world of smell, a world of hearing, a different sense of time, a whole other set of priorities, a sense of order and a set of rules and behaviours, many of which revolve around me and my behaviours.

So looking at an animal means always remembering the animal is looking back, seeing me as human. What does that mean for them?

I believe it is possible that humans once shared a non-sentimental relationship of genuine equality with whatever animals were near. They ate animals or were eaten by them. Hunter-gatherer humans lived closely with and among all sorts of animals. They looked and watched and paid attention to animals to see how they were behaving; if they didn't look closely and watch their every move and understand their language, however it was being communicated—by an ear twitch, a stare, a crouch, a noise—they could die or starve, and the animals undoubtedly looked back at humans for the same reasons. But not all of this looking was negative. Much of it was merely accepting the presence of another. People knew them in a true sense, not so much through naming but in terms of behaviours and use and movement and threat and communication.

According to the myths and legends, which sometimes make for uncomfortable reading, humans and animals also sometimes intermarried and seem to have been able to communicate in ways that are now lost. In fact, there seems to have been a lot of interrelationships, a lot of ways of interbeing, between humans and animals that have now been lost entirely. In many Indigenous stories, animals are seen as the teachers and moral arbiters of human behaviour.

What we have now, when humans look at animals is a hunger for contact on one side, but with little knowledge of what contact might entail, and an evasion on the other; witness the cars piling up on the side of the road at the sight of a bear in a park scrounging for some spring dandelions and fresh grass roots. The people are not only looking but taking pictures, memorializing this moment because it might never come again. They might never in their lives again see a bear in a situation where they feel so safe: close to their cars, in the company of so many other people, with a ditch between them and the bear, the bear obviously preoccupied. Alone in the woods, their reaction might be very different. Because they feel safe, they act as if the bear were tame, as if it were a zoo animal. They throw food at it; they shout, they demand its attention and are relieved they don't get it. Such an odd hunger.

Powerful contacts with wild animals are, in general, fleeting, fast, vanishing. But there is, often, that brief connection, an eye glance, a moment that feels significant when I see the animal and it sees me. The cougar crossing the road. The bear in the apple tree. The ravens that follow me all winter when I am out walking. The snake in the grass. The frog under the lettuce in the greenhouse. Constant. Instant. An odd sense of power trails me after that contact and I don't know what it means.

One night, Rosie barked, a high odd bark. I went outside, down the driveway to where she stood.

A large whitish coyote was standing near her. It saw me coming with the flashlight and didn't move. The three of us stood there in a circle of light and I asked her out loud, "Why are you here? This is not safe for you. You need to be afraid of people or they will kill you."

She stood up, moved a little way. Rosie followed the coyote. I followed Rosie. We went down the hill, across the large grassy field below my house. She kept lying down, and when she did, Rosie and I would stand still and watch her. Eventually, we got to the edge of the forest and I stopped. I said to her, "This is far enough." I called Rosie back. The coyote left. I had no idea what was going on. But there was no threat and no danger. Rosie was a huge woolly-haired guard dog. A coyote was not a threat to her. Nor was she ever afraid.

I went back to the house, puzzled. I am still wondering what her message was or if there was any message at all.

I try to not kill insects. Even mosquitoes. And when I kill them I take a moment to think of their small life disappearing so fast, into the dark. Wasps I love. They eat the aphids in my greenhouse. I am never sure why people love bees and hate wasps. They are pretty similar critters. And friendly, much more so than mosquitoes. When I sit on the deck, the wasps come and lick my arm, taste and smell me, then go on their buzzy way. I look at wasps, at their big gold multi-plex eyes. What kind of image do they have of me?

Perhaps it's about looking at each other without need, without hunger. Is it possible to look at any animals with no fear at all? No expectations? Only familiarity seems to create that sort of relationship where there is enough comfort on both sides for eye contact to linger. But even then, the predator stare can instill fear.

Is looking at domesticated animals always different than looking at wild animals? Are the rules established and clear enough for humans to really look at dogs, cats, chickens, pigs, goats, horses, and so on, with trust on both sides? But then we kill them. I often wonder if there was a terrible moment of surprise for them, after they had learned to trust me, after I had faithfully brought the pigs their dinner day after day, brought them greens and lettuce and other veggie treats, that moment when the bullet entered their brains did they think, "Hey, what the hell? Human?" Do we always betray animals? Must we? I don't know. But we do. Over and over, all the time.

Until fairly recently, the thinking on this point has been that scientists who want to look at animals can only see them one way, as non-thinking, non-feeling, non-emotional creatures, creatures who react to stimuli, who have instincts, but who are nothing like people. Now any sensible three-year-old knows this is silly, but science has stiffly maintained this attitude in the face of common sense, decency, and sheer basic kindness since Descartes—acting on the basis of no particular knowledge—told them to.

But now basic double-blind science is actually driving the point that animals and plants have consciousness, have feelings, can understand themselves, can use tools, probably have languages.

The problem is still language. What do you call that misty green fuzzy plant mycelium thing that might be communication among plants? Is it consciousness? Is it language?

We don't have a clue. We have met the aliens. They have been all around us from the beginning of time. It is so easy to make pompous statements about animals and everyone does. Everyone. And anyone who works honestly with animals ends up being humbled. Knowing in their heart of hearts that the more they know, the less they understand. That they know nothing. That they look into the deep brown eyes of the horse or dog they are working with, and the animal is probably trying hard to do exactly what this owner or trainer is trying to make it do, and the very mystery of that communication is shocking and heart-rending. Language. No wonder everyone keeps trying.

Such a small thing, a glance at Rosie, but she watches me. She watches my body and my eyes to see when we are going for a walk and where we are going. Since I got her, I have watched her try so hard to fit her huge rambunctious loud barking watchdog/guard dog personality into the rules of the farm. Oh Rosie, I think, even as I cajole and stare and say, bad dog, more for the benefit of the neighbours than her. Or I say "stay" loudly to keep her off the damn highway and thus alive and she hears something in my voice that convinces her that this time I really mean it. There is something dangerous out there, and she actually comes away and listens to me, even though her much better smelling and hearing convinces her that there is nothing there.

Someday we will, as Ursula K. Le Guin long ago predicted, decipher animal and plant languages. It will be difficult. But someday if we hear, as well as look, if we listen as well as assume, if we pay attention, instead of jumping to conclusions, we may indeed learn what animals have to say to us, even if it is only their body language we decipher—an ear flick, an eye turn, a nose wrinkle, a shoulder hunch, a tail swish. Or perhaps we will finally hear the swallows gossip, as they do over my head every summer, or we will know the true mystery of bee dance.

There is so much to know. We can look and look and listen and then lower our eyes and wait and watch. The seemingly simple act of walking around my farm, looking, walking with the dogs, playing with the horses, embeds me daily in a complex historical, ethical and cultural contradiction from which, so far, I have found no escape other than to live with these other beings with all the love and care I can.

The ethics of living with the non-human, and especially with animals, is a tangle we have only begun to unravel. Industrial agriculture depends upon us not looking, not seeing, upon the human non-human animal gaze being interrupted by walls and isolation. Looking at animals requires really looking, requires engaged looking, engaged seeing, engaged being with animals, engaged understanding. This is extremely difficult in a modern world where few people even see animals anymore or know much about them.

The opposite and opposing force to this industrialization of nature would seem to be vegetarianism or veganism. But the ultimate logical end of veganism would be to not domesticate animals at all, not to even have pets. But that won't work, in part, because animals won't un-domesticate themselves. There is now research that indicates that dogs, cats and perhaps horses and other animals, chose (whatever that word means) to be with humans. From their point of view, as far as I can understand it, that makes perfect sense. Humans offer both protection from other predators and a source of food. Animals are intensely logical. Whatever extends their life and makes them safer is something they will take advantage of. Living with predators has its disadvantages as well. Sometimes they turn and eat you. But when this is seldom and the advantages outweigh the disadvantages, it makes sense. So if they won't leave, what can we do but try harder and much more clearly, to understand this relationship?

Understanding this also, in part, solves my ethical dilemma about eating meat and riding horses, although it still leaves me uneasy. If I am a top predator, that is a position I am stuck with, however I feel about it. If animals react to me as a predator, as a food source, as a protector, as a force to be dealt with on their terms, it is a position I have been born into through evolutionary forces. All the sentimentality and friendship and petting and sweet treats in the world won't change that relationship. And it leaves me and all other humans in a huge welter of responsibility.

My cat sits on my chest at night, kneading my skin with her paws. Her blue eyes are luminous; she purrs and kneads in some kind of cat joy that I can only guess at. Her face has changed since she was first a kitten on my chest. Years of hunting mice and rats and birds have given her a wiry tensile strength and power. She and I lie together listening to the rain. I am so grateful for her company. Chronic pain makes the nights difficult. The company of a small white cat somehow eases that distance. Why and how I don't know. I don't pretend to understand her. She is a cat, with a fierce life. And we are together for this brief time. How glad I am to have her here. How broken I would be by her leaving.

Ethics aside, my being with animals, my looking, my enjoyment of them is one of the most important parts of my life. I keep thinking and learning about them. And I may never resolve any of the deep conflicts I have about how we as humans treat animals. So I watch and walk and listen with whatever respect I can. For now, that will have to be enough.

Always There

A long while ago, a friend came from the city to the farm to stay for a summer visit. She brought her sweet little curly-haired dog with her. It was beautifully shining white, pouffed and coiffured; her idea was that the dog would stay in the house away from the big farm dogs and we would take it for "walkies."

But of course, a dog is a dog, and within a day or two, the pouffy girl was out romping with the big dogs, running through puddles and burrs, and chasing gophers in the pasture. When her owner demanded she come back inside, she refused. So we all went as a pack on long walks to the beach and partook in family beach parties, which, all dogs are convinced, humans organize just for them.

When my friend prepared to leave and put her now muddy bedraggled wee doggie in her car, she declared, "As soon as we get home, she's going to the groomer."

I saw the desperate appeal in the dog's eyes and silently said, *Sorry.*

On our farm there have always been dogs. In summer, people come to my beach to visit and usually bring their dogs. There is an occasional growl or two but in general, all is peace. Dogs work it out. I have only one dog now, but she is a proud and attentive animal. She is a black lab whose person, Julie, had an unexpected heart attack. When Sable first came here she waited for Julie for a while, and then one evening she came over to me, put her head in my hand and said, "Okay, I am your dog now." She is thirteen and a bit stiff, but she spends much of the summer nights chasing bears out of the apple trees and winter evenings warning off the coyotes.

Dogs have always come to the farm, sometimes as puppies, sometimes as strays, sometimes dropped off and left. My brother, who is my farm partner, always had a dog he parked with me while he went to work. Dogs, when they come here, figure out very quickly that this is a dog-friendly place and they relax.

And there is also a dog graveyard where our dogs lie, under the wild roses, waiting, so I am told, for me to come over the hill and join them in some rainbow land.

A good working farm always has a dog or dogs—such dogs have multiple jobs, mostly to bark at things, or herd things, or guard things. A farm without a dog is a fool kind of place. How would I know what was coming and going, without the dogs to tell me: a deer, a coyote, a bear, a raven, a squirrel? Farm dogs are just there, at your heels, they circle out, come back, check in and then out again. Taken for granted. Always there.

When I was young, our farm dog was Willie—he was always at my dad's heels, so much that we never really noticed him until he got old and my dad "put him down," the vernacular for shooting him.

We noticed him two other times, once when my dad ran over his head with the red Farmall tractor. Dad brought him in the house, where Willie had never been, and his poor flattened head slowly expanded and he came alive again. The ground had been soft, the tractor wheels lifted off the ground because of a heavy load in the cart behind.

He got sick one other time, and again, my father brought him in the house and we all stared at him, lying sick on the floor, paralyzed. Then a neighbour came that evening, found the wood tick embedded in his spine and our mother got a match and heated a needle and took the wood tick out; again, Willie came back to life and went outside into the dark night where his job was to bark and chase off bears and deer.

Other dogs followed him. We loved all of them. They were all part of our family. I went into the woods or to the lake every day. I always had a dog with me. Having a dog in the woods meant I always knew what was going on, where things were, where was safe, where was not.

The coyotes have always owned and managed the land around the farm. They hunt mice in the tall field grass in the winter. They bring their pups onto the hill above the beach in the spring to howl together.

The coyotes and the dogs have always played back and forth between the edge of the trees around the farm fields— into the trees, out of the trees. They knew and know each other well. One afternoon, long ago, I went for a walk through the forest bordering the farm along the trail to a hidden pond, one of my favourite walks. I had three dogs with me: my brother's dog, Ben, a huge Lab-Husky cross, renowned for his ability to swim for miles behind my brother's canoe, my own dog, Rebel, and my mother's dog, Mickie, who was the very first "pet" dog we had ever had, who got to sleep in the house, and consequently, was looked down upon and teased by everyone. He only loved my mother and snapped at the rest of us.

We were going up and over a sandy hill when suddenly, a mother coyote came out and barked at us, a peculiar bark, very sharp and high. The dogs' reaction was odd—they immediately put their heads down and backed away. I looked at the mother coyote standing in front of a hole dug into the sand, and I also put my head down and backed away and apologized, and the dogs and I went around the hill and home another way. I have abandoned three dogs in my life and each time it broke my heart. When I finally got into graduate school and moved away from the farm to Vancouver to attend university, I brought my dog, Kinmont Willie, an utterly faithful, brilliant border collie-Lab cross to the city, but he had been too long on the farm and could not figure out the territorial rules of this strange new place. I took him back to the farm, to the unkind care of my father. My wonderfully gentle mother had had a stroke and was now in a care home. My father was alone with only his dog, Timmy, for company.

I came back to the farm as often as I could. I had sold my car, so I begged rides, or I rode the Greyhound. I would stay for three or four days and when I went to leave, Kin would crawl under whatever car I was getting into and stay there until I had to drag him out, tell him to stay, and leave again. I would cry and he would cry.

Eventually I moved back home and we resumed our companionship.

I was the only human for him and had been since the people who had his mother brought him as a small pup, late one night to my house, and said, "The coyotes got all the other pups. If you don't take him, they'll get him too." I held him on my lap for a while. I hadn't told them I wanted a puppy. What I had said was, "If I ever get another dog, it would be one like this," but now I had him, or rather he had me. I had a strange disease that spring which none of the rural doctors I went to seemed able to diagnose; it involved painful swollen joints, fever, rash, nodules on my arms and feet. And exhaustion, pure deep exhaustion that sent me for a nap every afternoon even though I had a garden to hoe, a teaching job, books to write. I put the puppy on a sweater by my bed and curled up to sleep. I got up in the morning and he followed at my heels as I walked over to my mother's house. He followed me home and curled up at my feet and from that day forward, he was beside me. A puppy needs to walk and so we walked, down to the lake at night, or over the fields or around the farm perimeter. All that walking kept me moving, helped my joints, kept me from despair. He saved me, that attentive black dog.

The collie in him was tempered by the Lab, but when he wanted to walk, he would fix his eyes on me, and I would find myself pushing away from the desk and putting on my coat and boots without really thinking about it. A good collie always has the ability to shift things.

Despite being a physically strong, hard-working farmer, I often had trouble with my heart. Both my mother and my maternal grandmother had similar issues. My heart would fibrillate, or race wildly, but a trip to emergency would set it right. While I was still in recovery from the brain injury, I went to Vancouver to go to a pain clinic.

When I got off the plane to drive home, my chest began to ache and burn. I thought I only needed to rest. But rest, visits to the doctors, calls to the cardiologist in the city didn't help. I couldn't get an appointment with a cardiologist. The new doctor I saw in my small town seemed to have no idea what to do. I stopped eating. I did the chores at the farm, I fed the pigs and chickens, I took the dogs for a walk every day even though I was struggling to breathe. I lost weight.

Finally, one day my son came. He and my friends insisted I had to go right then, away, far away to a hospital and get help. I thought I would be gone a week. I thought my animals would be okay and I would be home soon. Other members of the family were there; many people came and went.

But they were my dogs and they went to find me.

One was Rosie, a dog I loved and admired because she came to me as a wild dog, a crazy dog, and she gave me her heart. She was a Great Pyrenees, a guard dog, but she had been left alone in a pen and never socialized, never taught anything until I got her when she was two years old. My sister brought her as a rescue, thinking I needed a guard dog for the bears.

My sister hauled her out of the dog crate and tied her to the porch post. She was skinny, shaking. She had thrown up in the crate.

I untied her and she snapped and snarled at me—hard, desperate, scared—and I just said, "Let me show you where you live." We went away together, over the field to the lake, she pulling desperately on the lead. We went to the lake so she could drink and wade in the water. She was almost crazy with the smells and the newness and just wanted to run and run, but we walked the fence line, and I brought her home and made a kind of pen for her on the deck. Luckily, she was used to being penned and didn't challenge its flimsiness, and then we set out to get to know one another.

She had never been in a house or up and down stairs, so that took a while and lots of treats. Eventually, she loved the house and she loved me.

It took a long time to convince her that people coming to the farm were not predators who needed to be driven away. One day, many people were coming to make apple cider. I tied her up outside just where the cars were coming and she barked and leapt and growled at each car, but everyone ignored her because there was much to say and much to do.

Eventually, when everyone was busy, I untied her. She prowled among the cars, then prowled among the people. No one really noticed her and she was clearly a bit mystified by all this. When someone leaned to pet her, she stepped back, and after a while she got tired of being ignored and went for a nap. After that, she began to learn that when people came, she could come in the house and get treats and pets from them. I took her around and introduced her to the neighbours. Now she had a lot of territory to guard. She and Tugwell Boots, my sweet black dog, quickly became pack-buddies and romped together.

I had six horses at the farm that winter; she was used to horses. She always came with me at feeding time. She had a special friendship with one of the yearling colts and they would play together, pounce and run and jump. One night the horses heard something on the mountain—heads went up, tails lifted at the threat. No one was eating.

"Rosie," I said. "Go get it."

She was off like a shot into the trees and the horses watched her go, heard her barking, and then, very quickly, she came back, her white plume of a tail waving. She looked at the horses and they looked at her, and heads dropped and everyone went back to the hay piles. From then on, she knew her job and her place.

But a Great Pyrenees has minds of its own and I didn't understand this. She decided that the territory she guarded included our neighbours, which worked all right until they had visitors, and when summer came the stream of visitors was too much for her (and me). She spent a lot of time on leash or in her pen, but when I took her out for a walk or brought her in the house, she would put her head between my knees and just stand there breathing, while I told her what a great dog she was.

While I was gone to the hospital for far longer than I had anticipated, Rosie snapped at a neighbour who was jogging on the highway. My brother put her down and then Tug, lost and woebegone, was hit on the road.

I was still in the hospital, struggling with pain and depression and exhaustion that I couldn't seem to get over, and then someone said, "Your dogs are dead," and all I wanted to do was go with them. It really seemed too hard to live in the world when I had failed both my dogs and myself, when my dogs were dead and it was my fault that I couldn't get well.

When I finally came home, the moment I drove in the silent yard and no dog came to meet me was terrible. But I adopted two other older dogs that came to me—another Great Pyrenees, Pearl, and Sable, a black Lab—and the wound in my heart healed a little bit. But never completely.

The three of us spent part of last summer herding bears out of the cherry trees, one particularly stubborn momma bear with a limping cub persisted but the dogs caught on to where she was coming through the field and headed her off.

Pearl died last winter. She was embarrassed that she was letting me down by not being outside, but she finally relinquished her duty and breathed her last at my feet in the late winter afternoon.

Sable and I walk every day. But she is also aging and fading a bit and for the first time, often sleeps on the rug beside my bed instead of going outside and chasing the deer and bears.

Will another dog come to me? Do I have room in my heart for their stories, their waving tails, their delight in the lake, in summer parties, in long walks at night? Of course. When and how this will happen I do not know, but I have this theory that if I go out at night under the moon and say to the sky, yes, I could take another dog, the next day the phone will ring, or perhaps a lost dog will trot into my yards, or perhaps someone will bring me a puppy and say, "This is your dog." Dogs are magic that way.

BREAKING SUMMER

My grandson Louis stands on the rock, squints into the sun. He is fifteen, blond hair falls over his eyes; he has long lanky legs, big shoulders, a skinny body. He pauses, then runs, leaps, hangs in the air, splashes into the deep black-green water. He has made it, the long jump off Redman Point—named after the red Ktunaxa pictographs on the rock face—a dare that everyone has gone through in their time. He crawls into the canoe, trying to act nonchalant, knowing the big dudes on the beach will still tease him mercilessly over not jumping off the high rock, sixty feet above the water.

My farm on Kootenay Lake in August is paradise. Bright sun, warm nights. Ripe peaches. A garden full of produce. The beach, a curl of gold sand circled by wide round rocks, there to be raced over by kids and grandkids. They are into the lake and out, diving, swimming, lazing on beach towels. Skinny brown bodies flashing with light and heat.

We do family dinners, late night walks under the moon, flowers and fresh fruit and friends. Every day I try to hold on, but it all goes by so fast.

The spectre of fall and winter looms no matter how hard I push it away. Every day, I remind myself to revel in summer, to just have great times with my kids and grandkids, to be in love with the world. I am getting old way too fast, and I want to make memories for my grandkids.

But summer always breaks my heart. Summer in Canada is the cruellest season. It makes April into a piker. Summer is really only two or three weeks long. At my lake, on the August long weekend, almost anyone who has anything that will float is in it or on it, floating or roaring around in circles.

Then there are two or three weeks of blazing sun and beach time. Everyone lazes in the sun, drinks beer or pop, eats strange food. Sure, a diet of watermelon, chips, pop or beer, marshmallows, and burned meat is good for you.

Until about the third week of August. Then people start talking about having to get back for school or work. They go silent and stare into the fire. The crowd at the beach starts to dwindle. By Labour Day weekend, I am alone at the beach. The chairs are still arranged around the firepit. There is an odd collection on the picnic table, a silver earring, a broken necklace, lots of rocks—some painted— bottle caps, goggles with broken straps.

I still walk to the beach every day and sit in the silence. In September, there are no boats on the lake. The sky is painted a bright and brilliant blue. The mountains are hazed by smoke from the wildfires that burned the mountains across the lake this summer and choked the bay with debris, turning the sky grey, the water black.

I come up from the beach every day in the late afternoon and turn on the news. A fragmented cacophony of voices breaks the silence. The news is harsh, often terrifying. The contrast is jarring.

I have friends in Germany who come here every summer. They insist that the Kootenays aren't real, that we all live in a dream world but the news from the real world shatters the beach peace. How can they both exist? This summer, we had a "heat dome," perhaps a preview to even hotter, smokier summers.

I care deeply about the real world too, and I worry about

what those wonderful happy children racing over the rocks might face one day. There's not much I can do about the world out there right now except read and write and pay attention.

I am caught between the beach and the future, between time and no-time. All my life, I have been political, studying, writing, and trying to understand how to live well. But for many years now, it has seemed to me that the world is full of noise. I don't want to add to this often crazy-seeming cacophony. I do linger on Facebook for a while every day and I appreciate it a lot. I like social media. I usually use the same tone of voice and politeness on social media that I would at any social gathering—light, superficial, nice. I am nice.

But that begs the whole question—how to cope or understand or even live with the world in a state of such frightening fragmentation where there is both the paradisial beach and the black muck of "news."

Fortunately for me, the mountains and the lake don't care—they have been here for many millions of years, reflecting each other while people and their crazy affairs race by. The deer and the bears and trout and osprey don't care, they have a living to make and food to find. So I can still go to the beach every day and dwell in timelessness, at least for a few minutes. Every day, I walk on the mountains, down to the beach, up through the trees, watching, noticing.

In the fall, the world turns to gold. The lake is hazed with smoky blue; the field grass bends to the wind, purple and gold and blue.

In the winter, the wind comes in snarling off the black lake water and tries to eat my face. The beach is black and white and grey, the mountains hide behind a cloud lid. The lake road is empty. No one comes to see the astonishing harsh beauty of winter.

I wait all year through the fall, the bleak winter, the glorious spring, for summer. I wait, wondering what will change this year. Will Louis still come? Will there be new young children to explore the beach for the first time?

I know the lake road will again become a madhouse of cars, motorcycles, and bumbling RV drivers. People will come and go from the farm every day—visitors, friends, family, people working in the garden, or coming to pick peaches. I will boil the kettle, fill the teapot again and again. Mugs will pile up by the sink. The afternoon sun will broil the earth and at night the bright moon will sprinkle the water with glitter.

It will go by in a roar again, the summer freight train, weighted with goodies and fun. Boats will race in circles on the lake, cabins will fill and empty again. It's a kind of craziness, the Canadian summer. There are ghosts behind it, like the troll faces in the beach rocks at night. Memories built and lived. Traditions. Whose turn this year to be the kid who jumps off Redman? Who will be the first to race up the cliff face above the beach? Who can still eat fifteen peaches a day? Who is it, this year, that won't come back because of work or study or change?

It's perfect and utterly evanescent, like the pattern in a dragonfly's wings as it hovers over my hand. Even as summer hovers over the land, the light starts to slide off the gold of the dry grass.

A time of hazed lovely intensity. Here, gone, treasured always. Once again, we will sit by the lake under the light of the moon and light marshmallows on fire. What else are marshmallows good for?

The grandkids will race along the white lines of driftwood, high above the beach. Parents will yell reflexively, "Be careful," even though they did the same thing.

And at night, I will lie down to sleep, sun warmed and

sun browned, listening to the odd thud of the last ripe syrupy yellow plums drifting to the ground; listening to bat squeaks as the bat parade races around my house, devouring mosquitoes; listening to the last crickets sawing a tune in the tall grass by the garden. Waiting, again, for winter.

Summer. You rip me apart, you really do.

GIVE PAIN A VOICE

Heartache

Some days my body feels familiar and trustworthy, the same as it has always felt. I am the same, until I stand up and then have to sit back in the chair to breathe. Breathe, rest, get up again.

That's the trick. Some mornings, I work in ten- or fifteen-minute increments, then I can stay standing, breathe, puff and pant. Other mornings, I charge on, sending emails, writing, making phone calls, reading, taking walks around the garden to talk to flowers.

I hate old age. In my secret broken heart, I rage against it. I push my body hard and it pushes right back. Pain and exhaustion: Fuck off, lie down. Go die of boredom.

There is a secret language that goes on among us old, older, aging, senior, whatever the term is. It has no real words, other than muttered clichés. But when you tell someone about a new pain, a new diagnosis, the latest unhelpful thing your doctor said or did, a particular look passes between you. All you can do is shrug, say, good luck and head out. You know the drill now. But you didn't before. No one told you.

People head into old age as naively as teenagers heading into puberty. The car accident that I never recovered from precipitated me into an early old age. My heart wouldn't keep a steady beat. I kept going because I thought I would go right back to my old self, the twelve-hour-a-day working self, the one that farmed and wrote and stayed up late, working. What I didn't realize was that age had dug its claws in and was dragging me around by the head.

After seventy, you are mostly done with your life and you know it. But in various ways, you manage your time so it still has meaning. You cling to rituals of pleasure and endure the long moments of pain and exhaustion. You learn how to live with less and to live for now. It's a steady procession of loss.

Aging has stolen big chunks of my life from me. Death has now taken so many of my friends. It's weird when a friend dies. I notice and then the waters of daily life close in again and that friend is simply not there, the way they would be if they had gone on a long trip.

One of my closest friends in the world died before he and I were really old. We were in our fifties, powering along, both in a good place. We had both found the places where we had wanted to be for a long time: I was in grad school at last, and he had just gotten elected to political office as the regional representative for our area. We were happy and well and working at what we loved.

When he phoned to tell me his arm wouldn't move, I tried to make a joke out of it. That was before I knew what I know now, that any symptom is ominous, that things can go wrong and then get worse. Your body still tries its damndest to heal when you are older, but it's an uphill job; all kinds of things fail and break—knees, hips, hearts, new inexplicable symptoms show up at which your doctor frowns and suggests anti-depressants, or—in one case—reading a book about people who have imaginary illnesses.

But Alan went to the doctor and it was a brain tumour, an invincible brain tumour that ate him up and then wracked the core of his family away as well, so they scattered in sorrow and grief as they tried to make new lives.

After he died, I had a vivid waking dream, one of those dreams that you are convinced is real. Alan had indeed gone on a trip. We met in a train station, each of us catching different trains. We got coffee and sat down. I stared at him. He looked great. He saw me looking. "I'm fine now, I'm all better." God, I was so glad. We only had a few minutes together and he went off to catch his train. I think he might have been going to Morocco, a place he had once visited and loved. I was so relieved when I woke up.

I told his wife, who burst into tears. "I want to have that dream," she said, but never did.

And then much later, I had a car wreck—someone drove into me and I thought I would just bounce, and be fine, as I always have. Then I had another car wreck where someone else drove into me. My brain rebelled and went on strike.

Some medical person asked me once if I had ever had a bad fall, and I stared at her, stupefied, unable to think of where to begin. Maybe I should begin with the fall out of the top bunk when I was two, but then there were the many horses I fell off, the bikes I crashed, the time I fell out of the cherry tree, the time a full bucket of cherries flew off a ladder and hit me in the face. Yes, those times. Had I ever fallen? Let us not count the ways. Just ask another question, please. There have been so many of them. My least favourite: "Are you depressed?" There is no answer to it. Somehow that term seems to cover all varieties of human experience, from genuine madness to existential angst. Are you depressed. With no question mark. Because it is not a question, it's a lockbox with no air inside. Here, jump in. "We have drugs."

I think doctors are like police or social workers. They start off well with high ideals, determined to help people. Then they run into people who are mostly awful, especially when they are stressed, lonely, mad, addicted, vengeful, or just deeply sad.

Are you depressed? No, I'm exhausted. Yes, they look much the same. And someone hit me with a car. And now it hurts. And my heart won't work properly. But are you depressed? No, I am just really, really tired.

The least helpful advice I ever got from a doctor after complaining to her about pain, chest pain, not being able to breathe. "Take it easy," she said. "Stop trying so hard. Give up all those things. Just rest." What should I give up? My books? My grandkids? My horse? Reading and thinking? Everything central to my life that gives me meaning and a sense of Self? How does one do that?

My heart fibrillates. It never gets enough oxygen. The doctors tried to fix it by breaking it. They burned out the central nerve in my heart and then hooked me to an implacable, snotty pacemaker, a machine that makes me live. But they forgot to tell my heart it wasn't actually dead. For months, it raged and raced, sent messages to my nervous system and my brain: We're dead. Quit everything. Nothing ever quite quit but it was very confusing to be dead and alive at the same time.

Eventually, my heart settled down and then my brain did as well. Now some days, my heart and I are somewhat at peace; it grumbles away but keeps working. Other days, I sit in my chair, breathing and breathing while my heart pounds, wanting to jump out of my chest and run away, wanting to do anything but beat. But it's stuck with a machine, and I'm stuck with a heart that mostly works. It's frightening in an odd way. A pounding heart, sweating, not breathing, is what fear feels like. But I am not afraid. I just have all the symptoms of being afraid. I struggle to keep a distinction between the two. Some days, I agree with my heart. We should just quit. This is silly, all this pounding and breathing.

Other days, I laugh with the grandkids or stand with my horse, breathing and sighing together, the two of us; or I walk with the white dog, Pearl, and the white cat, Princess Snowie, to the lake under the luminescent skies of evening, lit from within by what Louis used to call "the godlight," when he was little and his other grandparents were taking him to church.

Other days, I write an essay, or I help someone else's book into the light of the world, not quite a midwife, perhaps a book doctor. Sometimes a book needs surgery. Sometimes it just needs a Band-Aid. Sometimes it needs a pat on the head and warm congratulations. Books come in all shapes and sizes. None are ever close to being absolutely finished. But the human story, in all its peregrinations, never fails me.

But other things fail. Cars, for example. Sometimes friendships. Sometimes families. Some families are good at coping with troubles. Mine are not so good. But that is their problem, not mine. And it means, most of the time, for most things, I am on my own.

Mine is this process so many of my peers have come to as well, which is living a life that has no future but has a good enough, for now, present. My present moment is one day long; evenings are transition into the relief of sleep. When I first got sick, I didn't sleep. The pain from my heart and my head joined together and got worse.

Now, when I wake, the first thing I do is check in with my heart to see how it's feeling. You'd think I would know but it takes a tea, and some breakfast, before I know if I will be able to have a real day, with people and activities, or a day in my chair, reading and working at the latest editing project.

It's not that I am ungrateful to my heart for working or to the many scientists and the work it must have taken to develop this truly amazing machine, which whams my heart enough to keep it flickering at seventy beats a minute, day and night. I don't know anything about this mysterious robot that lives in my chest. I don't even know what it looks like. I know the battery lasts ten to fifteen years.

I had a friend who finally had to have the battery in his pacemaker replaced. He dreaded the idea and when he told me about it later, I understood why. He said, "I could feel myself drifting away. I could feel the shock when they hit me with the paddles, six times, trying to restart my heart. Finally, it worked."

My battery is still good for "a while," according to the smiling, cheerful techie in the lab where I go once a year to have it checked. But I am pretty sure I don't want the battery replaced, don't want to die again and have to come back to life. Again.

Hearts have so many feeling words attached to them—heart-ache, faint-hearted, weak-hearted, downhearted, lion-hearted, failing heart, strong heart, brave heart—far more than any other organ. Hardly any descriptive words are attached to the brain, although I have always been vaguely amused by the term lily-livered (hard to picture that one). And there aren't a lot of other feeling terms attached to other parts of the body; snot-nosed is just literal, as is weak-minded. But the heart comes in for a lot of abuse.

Bits of research here and there show that there is an ac-tual heart-brain connection, but I doubt doctors would pay attention if I announced that I was "faint-hearted." Instead, I have "atypical angina" and "atrial fibrillation," meaning (I am only guessing here) that my heart is more like a big jelly than a strong muscle. So do I have a "quaking heart?" Am I now, "disheartened?" Do I have a "heartthrob?" What is going on in there anyway? Very mysterious place, the heart. Clearly, there is some connection between my brain and my heart, but I am not sure what it is.

Brain research says that there is increasing evidence about the brain-heart interaction. So when I am feeling "faint-hearted" or "downhearted," unable to move, feeling my heart buzz instead of beat, sitting in my chair watching the slow varied movie of light on leaves, of cloud shadows on the lake, it is hard to remember that other days are full of action, movement, joy.

Clearly there is an emotional component that I also don't understand, because on the days that are filled with children, people, words, I keep going, laughing, talking, until I come home. Then the shadows close in. I am not lonely, I am not afraid. I lie in the comfort of my bed, my home, the farm, the white cat on my chest, the white dog at my feet. The lake, the mountains fold around me. All familiar and beloved. And on the edge of something, the moon and stars and the darkness beyond. I sit on the edge of the unknown, the unseen, thinking of my mother, thinking that I want to leave my soul and spirit in this land and then be gone.

And all the while, my heart aches and pounds. I sweat and breathe and finally it relents. There is a stack of books beside me, a computer full of reading, movies, friends. Finally, it is late enough to take the pills, fold down the book, turn out the light, nudge the cat over to make room for my legs, and lie in the dark, heart still fretting and pounding and finally drift away, into an enormous darkness, full of dreams and silence.

Insomnia

One fall night, I went for a walk after dark. My dog had been barking louder and at a more ferocious rate than usual. My cat was outside but not with us. She usually walks with us. I grabbed a flashlight and walked down the driveway. Pearl ran ahead and began barking again, a real note of anger in her voice. We walked in a big circle down to the road and back up through the garden. By now, she was staying right at my heels, which she never does. And then I heard it, the soft *churrup churrup* a cougar makes when it is out and about. I went back to the house but there was still no sign of the cat.

Had the cougar taken it?

I went to bed but not to sleep. I read and went out periodically to look for the cat, getting more and more frantic as the night wore on. She came inside along with the morning light. She came in growly and spitty but alive. The next night, I made her stay inside and I could finally sleep.

When sleep left, it was a sudden shock. I didn't slowly lose sleep; instead, one night I climbed into bed—my head pounding with pain, my ears whining—hoping desperately for sleep to come and wrap its dark arms around me and make me better, and then it didn't come at all. I got up about midnight, head still humming with noise and pain, and had a hot bath and a cup of tea and then wrapped myself in a quilt. I probably slept although I wasn't aware of it.

After several nights of this, frantic, I began reading. I bought drugs labelled *sleep* from the drugstore and the health food store. I began to drink wine at night alone, which made me feel strange. Wine was for parties and friends, not for dark nights and migraines.

I wandered my way through this strange new world asking doctors useless questions. One said, "Well, maybe you have a sort of electrical storm in your brain." Not a helpful image. Mostly they just looked at me and shrugged and suggested endless varieties of anti-depressants, which sort of worked until finally, I found a combination of pills that mostly let me sleep.

And here I am. Still taking them, still fighting the elision of sleep, how it comes in slant, sometimes a surprise, sometimes a mongrel stranger, wandering into my room and slinking into my bed so that I remain craven, begging, on the edge of sleep, holding on, still holding on. Sleep and I are not friends. We were good friends until the car accident and the brain injury. Then sleep left. The sleep drugs work unless I am stressed or worried or upset or over-adrenalized because I have actually had a great day.

Sleep is a tricky bastard. There are also the nights I go to sleep peacefully, smugly contemplating a reasonably accomplished day: some writing done or some editing, perhaps a useful conversation with a writer, some words sent away, some words received.

And then other nights I lie down to sleep and discover that a conversation from the day is still sparking like an electric wire in my head. Perhaps a new idea, or a poem or a journey. It doesn't matter what it is. It matters that it won't turn off.

The brain is a hard thing to command. I can coax my brain now, when I have forgotten something, like the name of a book or a writer or a friend; I can put the question about a forgotten item into the whirlpool hidden somewhere in my brain and it will pop up suddenly, as if a sturdy little beaver down there has dug it out of the muck.

But sleep, for reasons no one understands, runs away when you try to catch it. Lying down and silently arguing with my brain and giving it orders to sleep, sleep, sleep, is counterproductive. The more upset I get with my contrary buzzing mind, the more awake it becomes. So I have to go softly, find distractions for it, perhaps reading, and more reading. Sometimes I think, okay fine, I will just read all night. At which point, my brain relaxes because I am not trying to tear a hole in it, and I fall asleep.

For people with chronic pain, who have difficulty sleeping, the worst time is lying down at night and waiting to see if sleep will come. So I dread the night as much as I look forward to it. Sometimes sleep comes slowly—I breathe, I wait, and gradually, flashes of dreams, wafts of memories, disconnected images show up. Sometimes I remain half-asleep, half-awake. If nothing interferes with this state, I will eventually fall asleep.

But the dog barking, a sudden worry, or sometimes no reason at all, sleep won't come. When it doesn't come, I get up. I make tea, sweet and milky, sit in my soft chair, turn on the radio, try to read. When I start reading the same sentence over and over, I sit back and try to sleep. Usually this works, sometimes it doesn't. It's two in the morning. I need more drugs, and quickly, because if I don't sleep, tomorrow will be hell. Headache hell, muscle ache hell. But they count my pills at the pharmacy—well, I think, I'll fool them, a half of this and a bit of that might work.

According to Statistics Canada, 50 percent of Canadians have trouble sleeping. I am far from alone—but so many of us are here, alone in our houses, in chairs, staring at television, or reading or listening to the radio or staring vainly into a dark space.

Sometimes, I find someone on social media who is also awake, but what can we do or say for each other? "Can't sleep."

"Me neither."

My mind goes to difficult places at night.

In winter, the cold comes down like a fist, crushing me, my tiny house, my cat, my dog, squeezing me until everything feels too difficult to manage. At night, when it's really cold, I am reluctant to take my pills and sleep. The pills take me down into a place of dreams that feels dark; old fears lurk there but only inside. When I go outside and take the dog and cat for one last walk around in the dark, the cold is less terrifying, it is only cold after all; the starlight (if there are stars) flashes on the dimly brilliant snowy slopes of the high mountain. Light from my flashlight blinks and echoes from various road signs, car reflectors, the neighbour's windows. Lights at night, glints and sparks. If I turn the flashlight off, the road glows faintly and I can walk (carefully) without it. When I was a child, I loved running in the dark. Running in the dark felt like flying.

Now I worry about stumbling over some unnoticed bump in the road. Apparently, the inability to see clearly affects your sense of balance. But the more my eyes adjust, the more shades of grey appear. I can see flashes of Pearl's white coat. Plus, walking wears me out quickly. So usually, finally, I can go back and sleep.

Sleep, we are told, is healing. Sleep is when your immune system kicks into high gear and makes your body better. Sleep is apparently when a host of tiny brain scrubbers equipped with dustpans and scrub mops and dust rags goes to work and makes your brain shiny clean again. The drugs I take are not good for my brain. The occasional shot of whisky at two in the morning is not good for it either. So, what to do? What a paradox. The things I take for sleep are not good for sleep. But they work.

But without sleep, I will drag myself through the day, working but without fire. Working but without the energy that I need. Writing is work. For a person with a brain injury like me, there is a thing called neuro-fatigue, where no matter how badly I need to, my brain won't create, won't come up with new words, won't round up ideas and join them into some kind of coherent sequence that will make an essay, a story, a poem, or a book. Without work, I am nothing. Without sleep, I am also nothing.

When someone is brain-injured, it means their brain has been bruised and hurt in some way. There are many kinds of brain injuries, from sports, from car accidents, from falls, from strokes, from any way in which the brain can be shaken and torn, so it turns into some mysteriously invisible kind of spaghetti, where the bouncing flashes of neurons, of thoughts and impulses and sensory stimuli and feeling, and all those bits of brain pasta must make new pathways and new connections.

My brain seems to have found new long-distance pathways looping thought to thought, idea to idea, but it takes energy to keep it spinning. When I spend a day with friends or my writers' group or at a book launch, I am just fine, chatting and laughing. In front of an audience, I light up like a talking doll, all flashes and hand waving. It's only later in the dark or the next day, as I sit in my chair, struggling with the computer and the alphabet to find coherence within language, that fatigue takes over and shoves me deeper into my chair to wait it out, wait for the little neurons to find each other, the flashing lights to come back on and light the way.

All day long, I can manage to appear and even be rational, smiling and working and chatting, taking grandchildren to the bakery or the library; and then at night, slowly, bit by a bit, a chemical fire grows in my brain and turns me monstrous. With neuro-fatigue, brain fire, whatever it is called, I have to take pills to douse the fire. Douse everything, knock my rebellious brain sideways, into a cocked hat, upside down and still murmuring, but somehow, magically asleep.

How I love you, sleep. Sleep, you dirty dance-away healer, I took you so for granted for most of my life. How easy it once was, to climb under the quilts, curl my arms around my shoulders, fantasize about being on a horse, riding away, riding away, and sometimes a few words would come, and I would drift into sleep, into dreams on a wave of images and colours.

HEAD ON FIRE

The woman on the other end of the phone line who once was my friend says, "Well, I have aches and pains too, but I don't let them ruin my day." I want to leap down the phone line and yell at that woman. Instead, I tell her calmly I can't talk to her right now because my head hurts. Then I hang up. By hurts, I mean, it feels as if someone has wrapped a rope around it inside, pulled as tightly as possible and then set it on fire.

I am raging inside, but I lie down, wondering how to survive the day and the pain and still do the things I have to do. I do stuff in spite of and with the pain. The physiotherapist told me that movement nerves are faster and stronger than pain nerves. So I believe her. I believe I can outwalk, outrun, outride pain. Sometimes it works.

Lying down doesn't make it better. Keeping going sometimes distracts me enough that I do momentarily feel better. But the price of that is exhaustion. Which means sleep, which means more pills. So, in general, I keep going; today, for example, my day includes a riding lesson, dinner with a friend, a talk with a book club and finally, blessedly, relievedly, home. Letting go of the effort of keeping going, of staying upright, of smiling, talking, maintaining some semblance of continuing to be me. By being me I mean a simulacrum of me that I put in front of me on bad days—something that walks and talks while behind it I rage, immersed in pain.

Pain brings powerful emotions with it, not just rage and depression, but joy and sorrow in equal measure. Some days

I wonder why I bother to keep going. In pain, I walk around saying both hello and good-bye. How can I live with this fire raging inside my head? How can I not live in this world of such beauty and pain? This world that wants to go away and leave me. Death, to me, doesn't feel like me leaving. Instead it feels as if the world will leave me, as if I will be left here alone, standing in the dark, left in a specific place, maybe on the road below my house, by the pond, with the frogs and the gophers and the muskrats—the world and its inhabitants, disappearing, leaving me alone the way I am alone at night, walking by the pond on my way to the beach and the lake. Left there on the road in the dark. I think of death as the world leaving me, not the other way around.

Without the things I need to live. Without the dogs running ahead of me to inspect gopher holes. Without the wind beating in off Kootenay Lake, the wind coming down off Castle Mountain, the green fans of the mountains behind the farm, this walk I take every day, the great shining beauty I first saw at five and didn't know it was beauty because I had no words for it but knew it was love. All this wants to drift away and leave me lonely in the dark. That is what death is. And then how will I get it all back if it leaves me there? My only consolation is that perhaps my mother will be there somewhere in the dark to hold me, but she will be as lonely as me. She always was.

Oh pain, the places you call me to, the murderous rages, the sorrowful joys, the nostalgic afternoons, lying in bed listening to music that calls me back and back into the dusty, deeply buried library stacks of my life memories.

The moments that pain calls me into rage are less than pretty but now mostly contained. I haven't murdered anyone. Yes, I do rant but only occasionally. And yes, in pain, I do, often give in. I lie in bed instead of moving. I lie still and read the news online instead—not a good thing to do, not a recipe for peace or joy, but a recipe. I keep on hoping, for seeing, for understanding, for something to do about it all, in pain and broken at seventy-one. Eight years of it.

Still, it is a recipe for frustration, and yet there is, also, within this reading, perhaps some kind of peace. The world rages on, and I am such a molecule inside it, a walking molecule in pain and also in love with light, and yet death and pain rage on within my head and within history and all around me on this small planet raging its peaceful way around a cosmos I cannot begin to see and understand. What can I understand, stuck as I am within the limits of my brain and my senses? Perhaps when the world falls away, then true seeing can begin? Or perhaps it is only darkness. And perhaps, my mother's hand, reaching for mine.

And reading the news lights my head on fire as much as the headache does and I am just as helpless. What is odd is that I am quite sure that many of us these days walk around with our heads on fire but we don't talk about it. Instead, in this world right now, we live in this void between seeing, understanding and acting.

Mostly we, my friends and I, live in right now. Which is a nice place, very nice so much of the time. The sun shines. The weather is a bit odd and changeable, but our friends are all here. We drink tea and go to lunch. We have lots to eat. The children we raised, the children we love so much, our children we raised to run in the sun, in the tall grass, to swim in the lake and eat the food that we told them was healthy (while they secretly craved the bright orange and brown of Cheezies and coke, the flatulent puffiness of store-bought anything, as long as it came in bright blown-up bags, and bright huge plastic bottles) are away now and working hard in the world.

Our children grew up in a world of dire prophecies where their mothers marched against nuclear war, against 2-4D, against racism, against environmental devastation. And now their children's children, our grandchildren, are growing up in a world filled with bright puffy toys, screens full of bright colours. They are growing up amid dire prophecies of collapsing glaciers and acidic oceans and climate change and dying polar bears, stories their parents don't tell them, yet. There is no way to make sense of this void and as far as I can tell, no one tries. Or do they? Is it me and my beloved long-time friends, and a few others who talk in secret ones and twos over lunch about our fear, our terror, our hope for this world, despite our aging bodies, our pain, our backs, our knees, our teeth, our eyes, all failing us when we need them most?

The absence of conversation, or even a newspaper article or two after the International Panel on Climate Change publishes yet more and more papers detailing, in ever finer and more comprehensive detail, the doom of this particular climate era and thus the need for the further adaptation of our nutty human species is amazing and even admirable. What does it mean to read a headline over my morning coffee that pesticides have poisoned most of the world's arable land? Well, on one hand, of course, immediate resistance and denial from governments and farmers' organizations and chemical companies. Accountability? Admission? Culpability? Never.

I have no doubt whatsoever that amidst great wailing and disturbance and collapse, humans and other species will somehow adapt. Nature is both resilient and adaptable. We human beings destroyed much of our own infrastructure and died in huge numbers during two world wars and then re-built the infrastructure and our numbers and carried on as if nothing had ever happened, determined, in fact, to recreate the world as it had been, only bigger, with more buildings. And bigger bombs, that the military isn't allowed to use. A mad world that has only become madder. And less easily in-fluenced by worried grandmothers.

A world with its head on fire. A world where everyone walks around pretending there is no fire.

As do I. In love with this moment and its beauty. It's an oddly lonely place. Did we do this, our generation? Did we not see it coming? Can I do anything now, with my aging crippled body, other than love what I see? Can I march, organize, make speeches? I did that, and yet, we are here. Many people are marching, organizing, making speeches, writing books about climate change. Not me. Perhaps all the marching and orga-nizing and speech making will, one day, be enough. But I can't tell and I will probably never know.

I am not a fan of counselling. I have never quite understood what it's for. It is a little too close to complaining for me. But at some point I had a chance to spend time in a pain centre and part of that time was spent talking to a psychiatrist. She was a lovely woman, and she asked interesting questions. Our process quickly turned into her asking me questions and me going away to write a two- or three- or ten-page essay in response. The questions began in a fairly standard way: What does your pain tell you; How did your family handle pain when you were growing up?

But then they got a bit wilder. I discovered or she told me that her true love in life was singing classical music, which she was still studying. We discussed music and great sopra-nos. I wrote about how my mother used music as her defence, not just against pain, but against the life she had chosen as a poor farmer's wife.

And then, on the next to last day I was there, she asked me whether visual beauty was important to me. Such a simple question. Such a silly question. Such a strange question. I walked around the west end of Vancouver in the rain for two hours trying to answer it. It was far too big a question to answer. When had I even noticed the world was beautiful? When did it start to matter?

Always, I concluded. I had always known. Maybe even before I was five, when I had that moment by the chicken coop, maybe the world has always been beautiful. And then when I was older, my mother taught me about music, sat me down, told me to listen for the stories within the music. So I understood that music was also important and beautiful and music contained stories.

I learned very early to run to look at the lake. I looked and looked. How amazing it was. Every day the water was a different colour. In the afternoon, the sunlight bounced and shimmered and reflected off the granite walls and buttresses of the lake rocks, the golden lake beach sand. The creek murmured over the sand. The creek could be dammed, diverted, made into pools, bridged. There were giant logs to run along or smaller logs to shove into the freezing water and pretend they were canoes. I loved the long white stretchiness of the logs against the smooth granite.

Nothing mattered on the farm if it wasn't worth money or we couldn't eat it. And yet I wanted to do something with the beauty I saw around me. I had no words for beauty. I was only feeling my way towards what I knew I wanted and needed, head on fire with stories and images and need. And then finally in high school there was poetry and theatre and English class with the one teacher who told me I was a writer, which was all I needed to hear. I realized I could put music and the colour of the lake and sound of the water and the stories the symphonies told me and everything else I knew into writing. And so, slowly, I began to learn how to do this.

After the psychiatrist asked me this question, for a whole day I struggled to find a way to weave together the words to explain the overwhelming importance of beauty, not just visual beauty, but beauty in every aspect of my life. I thought about the poem I had read by Wallace Stevens when I first started studying poetry. "Death is the mother of beauty," said Stevens. Is that why, when I walked to the lake every day, death sat on my shoulder and waited for me in the road? Is that why my head burned with words and images and ideas and thoughts as I walked?

But even so, when I wanted to write about beauty for my friend the psychiatrist, I found myself almost speechless with astonishment. Such a great question. It lit my head on fire in a whole new way, not with pain but with light and memories and questions. But beauty couldn't save me from pain.

The deer come down to the beach at night. I see their tracks in the sand or the snow. Sometimes they play, their tracks dance in the snow. My dog and cat seem to love the beach as much as I do. Coming down to the beach means the world opens up to me as my eyes and body are flooded with light. It's easy to take photos that people like at the beach. Something about the way the rock shapes replicate the line of distant blue mountains; the way that light reflects off the mountain peaks onto the water; the colours, blue- green- black-speckled granite, full of faces; the gnarled, twisted complexities of driftwood. Pearl is a solemn dog, an older female, a great watchdog, but often anxious. But at the beach she plays, runs, chews on wood, and tosses it in the air. The cat treats the whole beach as a giant shitbox, but when she is done, she races up the rocks, poses on top of the cliff, tail twitching, then races down again, leaps over the sand. They appear to be happy, to play. Why would I question their behaviour?

The pain is better now, but it has given me a working acquaintance with death and a far deeper understanding of people also dealing with grief and illness. I walk in the world every day now with an iPad under my arm, not to be a photographer but to be able to put a frame around things I want to look at more closely—anything that catches my eye and makes me look twice. It's like editing for beauty—bringing to sight the particulars that make up this mass of beauty I walk within, never the same view twice. It always surprises me.

I balance my life between energy and rest, between reading and writing, between walking and sleeping, between friends and solitude. It slides back and forth as I continue, like water slopping in a bucket. Some days are hard, some days are easier.

When people ask, "How are you?" I say, "Great," and mean it when I say it. Then I take it back when I go home and lie down in pain.

But still, I nod at the mountains and the troll faces in the rocks and trees. So little I know about anything, so much more to learn. Head on fire, stuck in the sky, feet plunking in the mud or sand or snow—looking, still looking, puzzling over, and for, what this world has given me.

MEMORY

I snapped at my beloved son the other day. Usually we clunk along pretty happily when we meet, exchanging news about our day or his kids and where these kids need to go and what I need to know to get them there. But the other day, he said something about memory, and I snapped at him: "People my age have the dementia demon on their shoulder all the time."

And then of course, I started to wonder about that. I'm seventy-two this year. I'll be in recovery the rest of my life from the brain injury. My grandfather was "senile," or so it was called in the family then.

Everybody jokes about memory as they age. But after a while, the jokes get less and less funny. So far (as far as I can tell), I am doing okay. I have a detailed schedule every week: meetings with writers I am mentoring, driving the grandkids to music or other classes. I write, I edit. Last year I edited six other people's books through to publication, and this year, so far, five. By anyone's standards, I keep up a pretty good pace. I keep most of my appointments in my head and I don't miss them and I'm never late.

But fatigue and fear ride around with me anyway. I watch myself watching myself. Checking keys, phone, wallet, grocery store bags, library books. I give myself time to organize things before I leave the house, and still I will come back in at least once or twice to check the stove or pick up something that needs to come with me.

When I was first trying to cope with brain injury and a lot

of short-term memory loss, I started to coach myself through the daily processes of my life, from making coffee to driving. It was a couple of months before I even felt as if I could drive.

Once I was brain injured, everything seemed complicated. In order to do anything, I had to break it down into steps and then talk myself through each step.

Once I was in the car and had fastened my seat belt and started the car, I had to remember to concentrate on the highway itself. Things caught at my eyes like thorns, dragging my gaze away from the road over and over. I had to consciously snap it back and lecture myself to concentrate. Every car coming towards me was a possible catastrophe but I kept telling myself I had been a good driver, and I could drive.

I clung to the steering wheel, clung to body memory and the knowledge that I was, in fact, doing okay or at least that nothing catastrophic had happened, yet. Since my brain injury had been caused by two car accidents in a row, where other people ran into me, panic sat right in the car with me. I pushed it down and eventually it settled into a heightened awareness that I still use to try to keep people from running into me again.

I also had to talk myself through learning to cook again; that took some time. And then reading and writing.

Another big one was learning to shop. My first trip to a store was simply overwhelming. I left the store, shaky, with a blinding headache. The same thing would happen if I went into the rush of noise and heat and light and smell that is a coffee shop. Getting coffee sometimes even now seems too complicated to bother with.

I did get better. Memory came back, trickled in, bit by bit. My concentration, my sense of self, my ability to read and write, also trickled back. I worked at reading, worked hard at writing, worked intensely at getting it all back. My life.

I thought about my beloved mother a lot, and over and over, apologized to her in my mind, remembering how I tried not to be impatient with her as she aged, but I was. I hadn't had any idea what she was struggling with.

I lived across the yard from her then and we went for a walk together every day. As her memory started to slip, it got harder and harder for her to get out of the house. She wasn't sure what to wear, a heavy coat or a light coat? She became more fearful of cold, more afraid of falling. Should she wear a kerchief over her hair? Had she turned the stove off? In and out and in and out. The stairs were hard on her.

But she would finally be ready to come with me. And we never stayed out long because anxiety would overtake her and we would have to hurry back.

Now I live in her house. At night, when I'm tired, the stairs are hard for me too. Arthritis has set in hard now in my knees and hips and shoulders. It no longer hurts but it makes me clumsy.

I look at my array of coats and shoes before I go out, wondering which one to choose. Somehow, I have one each of five pairs of gloves. How did that happen? But I make a list of things to do in my head. I make a list of groceries. I review the order of stores and people and who I am having lunch with. I line them up and snap them to attention. All good. All there.

But sometimes at the end of a busy day, under the chilly white lights of the grocery store, my thoughts, while not wandering anywhere, have this odd blurry edge to them. I check. Yes, I'm fine. I have to line up, pay for groceries. Remember, remember. Where is the car? Find it. Finally, I am at home where everything is familiar and reassuring. I sit, drink tea, eat one cookie, check emails and look out at the slow-moving land, the slow-moving clouds, the ponderously moving mountains, the creek bouncing over rocks, the sleepy mur-murings of trees, one to another.

I sit in my chair and watch the twilight come. What did I do today? What did I miss? What have I forgotten? It takes a long time until my brain stirs itself again. Where have I been? What have I been thinking about? No idea.

All the memory tricks I taught myself when I was brain injured are handy now at seventy-two. Easy tricks. Park the car in the same spot at the grocery store. Check for my phone, my keys, my sunglasses every time I leave anywhere. But other things also have their tricks. Some things just won't stay. Sunglasses and socks. They disappear and no one seems to know where or why.

Now, finally, for the first time in my life, I understand the need for routine, order, and familiarity. Someone once told me I must hate lids since I never put lids back on anything. When I was a hard-running, working mother, student, teacher, writer-type person, lids, dishes, a clean fridge, came last in my life. When I got up in the morning, I didn't look at the chaos; instead, I picked up my coffee cup and walked across the room to go to work. But now I clean, I put things in order, then I go to work.

I have other tricks. Every morning, I make a careful sequence in my brain of what needs to be done for the day and at what point I can stop and rest. Sequencing is tricky. If I don't plan it out, I will find myself stuck in the middle of the floor, not moving. Then I give myself orders to break the brain jam. Sometimes it is simple: make the bed. Other days, it is a more complex sequence. Feed the cats. Make the bed and put more wood in the stove. Now you can have coffee.

It's easier now to do this alone. Every new person in my space makes new complexities which I then have to re-order. It can be, and often is, exhausting.

But as a friend asked the other day, how could I tell if it was brain injury that I was tricking into good behaviour or old age I was fending off? I don't know. There is no way to tell. If the tricks work for both, I'll keep using them. As long as they keep working. There is some evidence that brain injury can contribute to early dementia.

It's a big ol' bogey, that word, dementia. You can't even kill yourself once you get it. You lose control of everything. Even the thought of it is humiliation. Far, far better to die young and stay pretty.

Memory is also a huge issue for aging writers and for me as a brain-injured writer. I primarily write memoir although I have roved about through, under, over, and within various genres. I wandered a bit as a writer until I found memoir and settled down. And here I am writing a non-fiction piece about the tricks of dealing with memory—stable or fading or flickering, or all the various shades it shows me throughout the day.

I teach other people to write memoir as well. Invariably, when we begin, we have a chat about memory and its unreliability, about memory and that flickering, ever evasive concept called "truth," a word I try not to use.

Memory is what I have, what they have. Memory is my tool. I work to keep it honed and keen. But I have no idea if my memory is really working. That's the truly scary thing about memory loss and dementia. I watched my mother, her care, her worry, making notes to herself. It scared her a lot and she had no one to talk to about it, least of all me. I was far too caught up in my own melodrama, frantically trying to write full time and publish, and stay alive financially while I did it. My mother and I loved each other deeply, but it is only now that I am reaching the age she was when her memory loss started to send its grey crackling bony fingers into her mind, that I am beginning to really understand her.

After my brain injury, one of the odder sensations I had was that my mind was too small to comprehend the immensity of what I needed to function. Every day, it felt as if I were peering through the tiny peepholes of my eyes from this small box called my brain. My brain felt too small. At the same time, it often felt as if my brain was being squished inside my skull, that it was swollen and violent with pain from trying to bang its way out.

Mostly now this feeling has gone. But still, I watch myself, mistrustful, remembering the fallibility of both perception and memory. The feeling mostly comes back when I watch complex science documentaries. But then it's fun. There are so many things in the universe where I have just a glimmer of understanding. But it's fun to try.

At night now, I sit with my white cat, with a book, with the other consolations of my life—a glass of wine, a bit of chocolate and a notebook. Making worklists. Checking things off, writing yet another to do list. Could I be, would I ever be someone, without this work, these lists of work, these complicated entanglements of words and images that I arrange and rearrange? Outside, the bitter cold of winter bites my house so it creaks and snaps. In the basement, the fire in the wood stove also snaps and growls. Nothing reassuring outside of this circle of light. I try to send my mind out, out, over the sleeping fields, the lake tussling with the wind, the hissing whisper of snow, over the high frozen peaks, out into the sky, the stars, the terrifying immensity of space, and back down, over to friends, grandchildren, the multiple beloved spaces where I make my life. It is what I have for now. I make lists. I hang on to memories, shuffle them into order. When I was young, the high sheer granite rocks at the lake sang to me in the late evening sun. When I came in the house, my mother's face, so intense when she listened to music and sang along, while her thin blue-veined hands were busy among the pots and pans. My father's voice, loud across the fields, calling in the milk cows. "Coooo boss boss, coo boss boss." And then the basement door, *thunk, thunk,* as my father brought in wood and loaded up the furnace, the sounds that punctuated the end of every day, until finally, his feet on the stairs, and the day was over at last.

WRITING FROM FATIGUE

I can't go. I can't not go. Walking. Out in sun, wind, rain, snow, cold, heat. Doesn't matter. I need to walk and so does Pearl. It's going up hills that gets me, hills and mosquitoes, hills and snow, hills in heat, hills covered with leaves, my heart whistling in my ears and breath rushing in and out of my throat, whistling like a leaky pump. But I make it. I always do. Maybe one day I won't. It doesn't matter.

What matters is how much fatigue chases me through my day. What matters is staying ahead of it. What matters is packing my day full so that when fatigue and exhaustion catch up with me and flatten me entirely, I will have at least accomplished something. This of course seems counter intuitive. It would seem sane and sensible to parcel out the small chunk of energy I wake with each morning, slowly, to measure it carefully, as one would measure out meals or cups of tea. But fatigue, neuro-fatigue, doesn't work like that.

Many days I sit in the worn brown chair, the same chair my father sat in while he was dying, where he slept away his days, too lonely for my mother to be able to stand his life. He woke, ate, shambled to the bathroom, back to the chair and back to sleep. Sometimes, he would look around, say, "Why am I so sleepy?"

But he didn't try to fight this kind of sleep, as all his life he had furiously fought poverty, grief, work, animals, weather, and bosses. Instead, he let himself slip back into a comforting sleep. He had cancer, but it wasn't the cancer that killed him. It was exhaustion. A few times when I urged him to get up, to walk, to try, he looked at me and said, "What the hell good am I if I can't go out and get to work?" And so he slept as he had lived, by his own values. If you can't work, why live.

I sit through my more exhausted days, the days when it is hard to breathe and my heart sits in my chest like a lava stone, burning, whirring, and aching, but I keep working, and even so, by five in the afternoon, I have had it, my brain fizzling, empty of words and work. I get up and go for a walk, more like a toddle. Coming back up the hill from the beach, we all pause every ten feet or so, me for breath, panting hard, and then slogging on. The dog and the cat lie down on the path just ahead of me, the white dog panting in her heavy coat. I don't lie down, but I lean over, close my eyes, hanging onto the air, and straighten, open my eyes, go back to watching, always watching as the world unfurls around me in its endless fricative, fractal whirls.

What keeps me going is the knowledge that if I get a good night's sleep, not always guaranteed, I will reach tomorrow with enough energy to lunge through the day, from my riding lesson to a lunch with friends, to a meeting with a writer, and home to water the plants, feed the dog, and sit in my chair and catch up with emails and Facebook.

If it has been a good day, I will even have enough energy to make dinner and do some writing before collapsing in front of a bad movie. If the day has been overwhelming, I only sit, paging through and editing someone's book, or clicking through the internet, reading book reviews or political posts to make the hours pass.

Some days I just lie down, because even breathing seems too much of an effort. Being alive is too much of effort. My heart fibrillates, refusing everything. My skin burns and freezes. All I want to do is sleep, unlike my father, not to escape but to recover.

Such moments are terrifying. What if this is the time I don't recover? What if I finally become one of those chronic fatigue people, barely able to move.

But when I do recover, I get up, move on, forget the exhaustion for now.

I push myself hard, hard, knowing the fatigue will get me back, knowing that I can stretch my energy like a rubber band until it snaps back hard. It means I still get to have a life, with repercussions.

When I was a kid, I was tall, strong, broad shouldered like my dad. I don't remember being tired. I worked for endless summer days on the farm, and then after school all fall, all winter, all spring, I went up the mountain into the forest or to the lake, along the rocks and logs. I ran, I climbed.

My sister and brothers and I were always on the move. In the early summer mornings, we set ladders and climbed inside cherry trees, crawled out to the ends of branches, held on with our toes and fingertips to reach the last, highest cherries, and then I would carry two apple crates full of cherries on my shoulders, almost forty pounds altogether, from the orchard, then up the rocky path, barefoot always, and then over to where the fruit stand sat beside the highway, trying to catch tourists.

I don't remember tired—not even when I got old enough to count the miles and realize that my brother and I had run over eleven miles to round up our cows and bring them home. I do remember thinking that was a lot and being proud.

And then I remember being pregnant, walking along with my high wide belly held in front of me like a trophy. I remember children waking in the night. Over and over every night, two of them in diapers, one nursing, one needing a bottle and how my body, huge and strong and dependable, kept responding until one day I sat in a chair and couldn't force myself to get up, and wondered what was wrong. I stood up and sat down and stood up and sat down again until I finally found the energy to keep standing and realized, with some wonder, that I was tired, an unfamiliar feeling.

I remember running against time as a single mother with four kids and a bellyful of secret ambitions to be a writer, but growing a huge garden instead, trucking food to market, trucking groceries home, and finally trucking to university in terror and fear and finding my true home there instead.

I don't remember being tired but I remember anxiety. I remember never having enough money or enough time or enough of everything. I remember being wrapped around and around with barbed wire worries, so restricted that at night, in order to go to sleep, I stabbed myself over and over again with an imaginary knife that penetrated my heart and therefore, somehow, let me sleep.

In my family, we were never tired or sick. But my mother's heart also bounced a wild tattoo among her ribs. She tried to explain that after she got rheumatic fever, it raced too hard as she trudged through her day from chore to chore, so many chores, never completely done.

I can't even imagine it now, even though I did it myself. How did we do it all, all the growing and picking and preserving, all those meals cooked, devoured, dishes done, dogs fed, and my mother collapsing finally in front of the TV, a glass of wine at her elbow, her hands busy with knitting.

I don't think my father ever used the word *tired*. Even while he was dying of cancer, work was what preoccupied him.

Night after night, my brother would dream of our father, who appeared to him, and showed him the work to be done on the farm.

And my brother kept up the farm as long as he could. I would see him on a hot July day, as I walked by raspberry bushes and black currants dripping with ripe fruit, the garden strangled with weeds. As I huffed and puffed my way up from the beach, I would spy my brother on his knees weeding the potatoes. Hours later, he would still be there.

Why did we still do it long after we needed to? We were both able by then to buy anything we needed. Instead we carried on, true to what we were taught, true to our roots, our long ancestral line, the grim faces of the Armstrongs, riding and raiding their way among the hills of the border between Scotland and England; and on my mother's side, the Klingensmiths, building forts in the US against the Indigenous people—clanging-smith people, the smiths always the centre of any village, any fort, their huge muscled arms raised against the heat as they made the tools for the people to farm with, as they made the weapons for the people to carry to war, as they shod the horses and strapped iron on to the wooden wagon wheels that would carry people into new lands. The smiths, who never got sick and never got tired. If they got tired, they were dead because they couldn't work.

I don't remember being tired—even when my heart first began its wild shenanigans many years ago, bouncing around like a crazed drunk dancer, skipping and dancing so hard it forced me to climb stairs on my hands and knees. I was broken-hearted enough at the time, going through a divorce I didn't want, so the physical broken-heartedness echoed the psychological pain and merely seemed what I deserved, what I had earned in my stupidity and blindness and my wild careering ambition that led me to so many wrong places.

Before the pacemaker, the doctors fixed it and fixed it by shocking it, and my heart and I stumbled on until there was no more fixing, only the stumbling, the fatigue in the dark, that imaginary thin glass knife now firmly embedded up to the haft, never leaving.

And eventually, nothing left but this sidling across bits of energy, like stones in a river, always expecting to drown but still going. How there is always another stone, across the great deeps of sleep, that somehow allows me to continue.

And continue in some fear. Knowing that one day the next stone will not be there.

But tomorrow does come, always, (so far) over and over again, a miracle of light stealing ever so gently down the mountains across the lake and tip-toeing over the sand and rocks, over the grey slanted driftwood logs, over the cedar trees with their roots in the creek, over the grass and up the cliff edge to my house, squatted sleepy and murmuring to itself, on its high granite ledge.

And the miracle of forgetting; for some reason, brains don't really remember pain. You remember that you were in pain but not what it felt like. So at night, when the freight train of exhaustion rolls in and runs over me, I am always surprised. And in the morning I always think I am well and can do great things.

In this odd stumbling way, I live my life. It enables me to keep up. It enables me to rest. Balancing, a juggler of light and dark, exhaustion and exultation.

Give Pain a Voice

It was one of those casual encounters in the grocery store, a neighbour, not someone I knew well. I had seen her husband earlier. He stood at the entrance to an aisle. His face was white and his body thin. Community gossip was that his cancer was getting worse. I could see what that word, *worse*, meant in his face. I passed his wife with an easy, "Hello, how are you?" A standard greeting that means nothing. Or today, something.

"Fine," she said. "How are you?"

I am never sure how to answer. "Fine" is too big a lie. But no one has the time for details. Nor do I believe they want the details. So I usually say something like, "Okay," or "Middling," or "Surviving," depending on how well I know the person and my mood at the time.

"Fine," I say cheerfully. I'm in a hurry and it's only the middle of the day so it's not an unreasonable answer.

Except she stops me, looks at me and says, "No, really, how are you?"

So, I tell her, briefly, about the pain, the difficulty of getting through an ordinary day. She listens.

And then I say, "And how are you?"

She looks away. Her eyes well. "I'm okay," she says.

We talk. We're blocking the bread aisle. We don't care. She pulls an essay out of her purse on chronic pain that she has clipped from a magazine. She hands it to me. We talk intensely, our heads close together. We talk about pain and grief and related issues. People edge around us. Finally, we laugh and prepare to leave each other.

Then as her eyes well again, she says, "The hardest thing is, when my parents died, Dick and I faced it together. I always had him. Now I have to face his dying on my own." We hug and say good-bye with a special intensity.

Pain has a loud voice, and somedays, it is the only voice I can hear—the multi-toned, multi-coloured drone of pain. On such days, nothing exceeds it, not the voices of birds or the colours of the land around me or the kind and loving ideas of what to do from other people, people saying anxiously, I love you.

Pain has an appetite; it takes the good intentions, the advice and kindly ideas of caregivers, the beauty of the world, and turns it into rage and bitterness. It devours the good and takes who I have been away. It takes me by surprise even when I know it's coming, even when I fight—tooth and nail, head and feet—pain wins. Of course it wins.

I had a car accident and then I had another car accident, both in unlikely times and places, both clearly not my fault. My head ached; I stopped sleeping; sound screamed in my ears. I went to doctors, lots of them, and healers, lots of them— massage and physio and acupuncture and naturopaths. I paid them from my dwindling fund of non-working savings. The doctors offered what they had, which were drugs. They offered drugs and no diagnosis. They offered anti-depressants for the pain, opioids for the pain, anti-seizure drugs for the pain, sleeping pills to knock me out. I took them. Of course I did. I was grateful for them.

I still am. I stand at my bureau at night, I measure out my handful of pills for pain and insomnia and I am immensely grateful. I lie down, in the dark, eager, too eager, for unconsciousness. I wait for it. I try too hard to relax, to sleep.

Nothing more ridiculous than trying too hard to sleep. But the drugs are usually infallible and sweep me away in a few minutes.

But sometimes there is an hour of waiting, in the dark in pain. And then the falling away into nothing. Perhaps I dream. Perhaps not. The internet says the pills block real sleep, that I need REM sleep to heal. I don't care. I am only greedy for the night, and freedom from pain. To be unconscious, uncaring.

Every morning, I wake with hope. Some days I get up, holding my head still, like balancing a too-full mug of tea. And some mornings, I get through tea and toast and even the breakfast dishes and emails and even a few hours of work before the pain makes my head swell, a pressure from the inside, a slow fire building up from my neck, over my ears into my forehead. My head burning from the inside. There is nothing to do but push through and take pain meds. The pain meds shut down part of the central nervous system. One of them is called Gabapentin. Gabapentin influences neurotransmitters, which send messages between nerve cells. It makes me shaky, somewhat stoned, and forgetful.

But gradually, my head becomes just a swollen lump on the top of my shoulders, and the pain recedes. I can walk and talk but I'm faking it. I am somewhere far away, distant from my body and distant from my pain. Somewhere I have a body and a life. The lump on my shoulders smiles and talks for me. The noise in my ears is constant but distant. I function. That's what I want. That's what my doctors want. "Are you functional?" they ask. Meaning, can you drive, make tea and toast? Find your car in the parking lot of the grocery?

After the second accident, for two months all summer, I sat in a chair, not functional, in despair, suicidal, and raging at the arbitrariness of two car accidents that had stolen my life.

Kind people came and went but I was unmanageable.

Raging when the headaches came, pounding and burning my head. Not eating the food people brought and made for me. Dreaming of suicide. Suicide ideation, as the kindly therapists put it. Wishing to die in a way that wouldn't devastate my family, is how I thought of it. Drifting away on a raft in the middle of the night. Getting lost on the mountain and never found. Or the best, going in my sleep. Take me, please, please, I would say to death.

But death has its own strange rules and it ignored me. It took the tools of my life instead. One sunny summer afternoon, while everyone was at the beach, death came in, lay all over my living room like a dusty blanket, like a suffocating haze—computer, dead; books, dead; kitchen, dead. I sat in my chair and panicked until I heard the voices of people coming back to be with me. Death and its haze had left, but I knew it hadn't gone far.

I got up out of the chair to be alive again, to hear real voices, to see the faces of my daughters and my grandson.

Summer was soon over, and people had lives and I had pain medication. I got up and got in my car and went for a drive. I had to cook. I talked myself through cooking. I decided to make cookies. I used to like baking. I would make cookies for my grandkids. I told myself every move to make. Take the eggs out of the fridge. Now put them back. Now mix. Now turn the stove on. Now put the cookies on a cookie sheet.

Once the cookies were in the oven, I wandered away to the computer. Forgot about them until the smell of sugar burning warned me. For the next batch, I stood over the oven, waiting.

I made lists. I reminded myself of what to do. One thing at a time. Go to the bedroom for pills. But while in the bedroom, there were clothes to pick up. Maybe something in the closet to look for, then back out to the kitchen to make tea. What had I been going to do?

Yes, take pills, more pills please.

This from someone who had not long ago flown through a day of chores—writing, teaching, gardening, zipping from here to there, keeping track of a million details. Illness? Ridiculous. Who had time for it?

Now when I went out, I drove slowly and carefully, reminding myself to stay focused. When I shopped, I was conscious of appearing busy and determined and normal. A shopper. A person with a life.

And I watched myself, nagged myself, pushed myself. Determined, I tried to pick up all the dropped threads of my once far too busy life. I picked them up one by one and then pain got in the way. I sat in front of the computer, determined, and still pain sat between me and the screen. Some days I picked out one word at a time, set each one down, a line of words. Sometimes a paragraph. And another.

Reading came back too. I had spent a whole summer not reading. Unthinkable. But now, finally, I could read a paragraph, then a story, then a book. Lots of books.

But no matter what I did, or how determined I was, in the late afternoons, pain marched in and took over. I went outside and walked and walked, the dog at my side. I walked, light-headed, through glorious fall, my feet, far from my head, walking. I came home with just enough energy to fight my way through pain to cook some food. And then finally, gratefully, I could collapse into my office chair in front of the computer to watch and be distracted, watch anything—movies on YouTube, movies courtesy of the library, through every half-assed decent film on Netflix, watching the clock the whole way, wanting, more than anything else, to be exhausted enough for it to be time to take the pills, be gladly unconscious, again, for another whole night.

And so the fall went, and then winter. Each day, a routine dictated sternly by the limits of energy, the limits by my resistance to pain, by pain itself. When people I knew, kind loving people, saw me in the library or the grocery store, they asked, "How are you?"

"Not so good," I would sometimes say.

And each one would do the same thing, step back, look me over like a purchase they didn't want, say with enthusiasm, "Well, you're looking good."

To which I would reply, "Yes, thanks."

One day, a woman I didn't know well, stopped, held my shoulders, said, "Wow, you look great. You're so thin." It was true. I had lost a lot of weight. Mostly, food seemed repulsive.

Somehow, asking me how I was gave people permission to go away, to tell people how they had seen me and I was looking good. And left me with a mouth full of words that recoiled. Who could pain rage to? Who could hear such crap? And why would they stay to listen?

So, instead, we rage at each other, pain and I. It pounds nails into my head. When I read on Facebook and various listserves what other writers are up to, pain laughs. You can't do any of those things, you can't apply for that job, you can't do that tour, or go to that event. You can't do any of those things. You are off the rails. You are sick. You are dying. You are getting worse. You are in pain, and you always will be.

Pain takes away agency, control, ideas, initiative. There is my life, just over there, full of books, ideas, rational thoughts, research, teaching, walking, my garden, my horses. And here I am, caught, veiled and wrapped around by my pain, cocooned, eaten, but still alive.

Pain is my life partner now. Pain is as truthful, in its way, as booze. And just as big a liar. It tells sly lies, and it shines a light on my life in a way that nothing else has or does. A person in pain is not one person anymore—there is the person and then the pain raging inside. The pain is multi-voiced, bitter, vicious, angry. Pain, like booze, brings bitter truth with it, and even more bitter lies.

But the truth can't be spoken out loud. Who could withstand the acid voice of pain? Not me.

Who could argue with it? Pain can sweep away any argument, any soothing help. The voice of pain is a voice that screams for help, screams despair but wants control. Who would even want to be in the same room, in the same vicinity as pain? The person lives with this voice. It takes up all the space both inside and outside, I want to escape but there is no door, not even a crack for that fabled light.

Distraction, say the soothing caregivers. Exercise. Interrupt the cycle of pain and depression and despair. Reward yourself. Pain can be managed, interrupted, distracted, made plastic. Neuroplasticity. Change your thinking. Be positive.

Yes, I think, I can give myself rewards. I can find my books, my writing, my students, ideas, things to read, understand, think about. And there are my friends, waiting to be asked to go to lunch or come for a visit. There is my kitchen, full of recipes and baking pans.

And I could, I will, I do, get up, take pain with me like a cage strapped to my head, balance it on my shoulders, walk to the kitchen, peer through the bars, read recipes, get out flour and milk and eggs, make something. Sometimes I do just that and sometimes it makes me feel better. Distracted. Busy. Rewarded.

And when I sit down or lie down, the pain is still there.

Pain limits what I can do. But what I do has always been my identity. Work is who I am. I have panicked as this slid away. I must do this, I think frantically. I am a writer, I work with words, I read, I edit. When the pain hits hard, I wander around the fringes of writing, thinking about it but not writing. Maybe start an essay, I coax, or pull out a manuscript that needs work. But the manuscript has a hole in the story that I can't fix. I read it over and over and the words won't fall into place, the sense of it won't come. Slow, I think, go slow.

It would be easy here to fall into the pit. I can see the pit and I can hear its temptations: self-righteousness (you don't understand how it feels); bitterness (this isn't my fault, why is this happening to me?); fuck it (I am so sick I am just going to hurt/kill myself, drink, take more drugs, eat too much, or whatever other self-destructive behaviours will hurry this process along); self-pity (I am in the worst pain anyone has ever had and I need everyone around me to know it); or other variations of this pit.

This is very similar to the pit that I used to fall into from anxiety and depression. I always had reasons for the anxiety and depression; I was too busy, too poor, too lonely, too overworked, too pushed, too stressed. Now for the first time in my life, I'm not too busy. Instead I am in pain.

Except, there is no question that pain brings depression along with it, that physical pain and emotional pain are intertwined in ways that medicine and people in pain don't always understand. Expecting someone in pain to be cheerful is a double issue; they can't be cheerful because they are in pain, but part of pain is not being cheerful. How to win at this particularly iron-toothed contradiction?

"Winning," curiously enough, if winning is even close to the right word, seems to involve a certain amount of grimly determined cheer, a certain amount of exercise, a certain amount of whatever gives you joy, whether that is family or anti-depressants, and a lot of rest and recovery. And balance between that exercise and rest and recovery. None of this is easy and there is no guarantee of relief from pain. So a certain amount of sheer strength of character and will and determination comes in as well. And whatever will back up. Prayer? Bring it on? Positive thinking, fine. Massage, alternative healing, shamans? Yes, I'll take it, I'll try it, provided it isn't dangerous or costs too much.

Sometimes healing comes by accident. Sometimes it comes when you aren't even noticing. I walked myself out of arthritis pain over a period of ten years by just that, walking and having a life. My dog walked me, my work walked me, my busy life walked me and the arthritis pain lifted and went away.

I don't know if this pain will do that. It is ten times better than it was four months ago and a hundred times better than it was last summer. But every afternoon still, an iron noose tightens around my head and squeezes my mind down into a nub of itself until I give up, insert what is left of myself into a movie, and desperately hope for distraction until bedtime and those beloved pills. Time alone will keep telling this story.

I get through each day one at a time. I do the dishes. I make the bed. Chaos waits just outside that routine. Put things in place, in order, or I will never find them again. Dementia wiggles its crooked ancient fingers. When I pack for a trip, I get everything in order and then entirely forget to pack pants. Or another day, I write all morning with what energy I have and find out it was the old version of the manuscript and it all has to be redone.

My computer dies and I have no money for another one but I have to get one anyway. I am a writer. It's what I do. I need at least the tools of a writer, books, reading, a computer where words go in the keyboard and books emerge. Or they used to.

So my days continue, with moments of brightness when I emerge with energy from my mornings, determined to continue to be me. Moments when I retreat, defeated, into darkness and the small tinny relief of movies played on the laptop. Moments when death crouches in the corner of the room with its handfuls of black dust.

And moments when someone says, "No, really how are you?" and the pain flows into a bright electric path, lights up the connection between two people—shared words, shared understanding—however brief. I walk every day. I notice the birds, the leaves, the horses, the dog running, the cat at my heels. I notice I am alive. I keep on noticing. I say sometimes, to someone, "How are you?" and a bright silver line of words flows between us. "Yes, I know," we say to each other, "Yes, yes I understand."

THE WHITE ROOM

THE WHITE ROOM

The white room is a place I dream into being. Sometimes it is a refuge, sometimes a waiting room, or sometimes just a pause. An empty room, a bed, a table, maybe a hot plate. A big window looking west, streaming light. Perhaps the room is high up or low down. It doesn't matter. The view does not matter. Only that there is something to look upon so that the endless fluttery pageant of weather and clouds and rain and sun continues to pass, very slowly and always changing.

What to do here, watch and wait and sleep. And read. And write.

It is a room of such deep luxury, a room where no work happens, no striving, no competition, no ambition, no trying. The biggest effort is getting out of bed or not getting out of bed, drinking wine or not drinking wine, reading one book that stays unfinished and beginning two, or five, or ten more. Nothing will matter in this room. That's the trick. No meditation of any kind. Even meditation is an odd kind of discipline, a striving after nothing at all.

If words come, that will be something. If words don't come, someone will wait for them or hear them.

In the white room, there are no curtains and all the windows open wide. There might be a balcony or a deck. Or not. It's the chair that is important—the sitting and the seeing, the waiting. The bare walls.

Nothing is simple. The room is not about simple. The more waiting, the more difficult everything becomes. Even the waiting is complex, loaded with the possibility of purpose, of starting and stopping. Looking at the sky is always terrifying. The weather makes its own commitments, and no one know what this means.

Outside this room, the world murmurs in deep, profound conversation, the orange-barked pine trees send rumours and gossip to each other along the sparked mycelium, the grass makes its own story, and deep within the electrons and far beyond the galaxies, sparkled things spin and twirl in their own courses, and that story, what it's about, is written with dark materials and dark numbers and some kind of enormous and unknowable imagination.

What happens to dead things in a world littered with dead things? Outside the windows of this white room the trees breathe and die; sometimes water comes to them and sometimes it ceases, insects hatch and die in brief fluttering moments. Watch and see, that's what the room is for. No more pushing to know, to understand, to pull information and analysis together with words and more words. Words that live, are breathed in and out, words that swim, words that are joy, are playthings, are dough, are plastic, and some are sculpted into snow people, soon to melt into print and be gone. Lost then.

Because there is always a new story, drifting in on the wind, and turning into dust, so that the white room must often be swept and dusted. The one in the chair by the window murmurs to the night, to the moth on the curtain, to the heaped dust on the windowsill, to the words clustered in a halo around the lamp, around her face and tangled in her tousled net of hair. Ah, but the words are sleeping now.

And only the night is awake, electric with billion-year-old light, and the resonance of fire, glowing and snarling deep in the earth, snapping at its box of stone and iron.

How Language Fails

When he was about ten, one of my grandsons looked at me with acute hurt, distaste, and surprise, and said, "You exaggerate, Grandma." His face was screwed up in betrayal; his grandmother had shocked him. Not only did she exaggerate, she actually lied. He had just realized this.

How did he catch me? Clearly, some parent had said, "Oh that's not true. Your grandma exaggerates." And I do have a lot of stories I tell my grandkids about what terrible children their parents were, how their parents never wore clothes, never went to school, and ran away to their grandma's house to eat toast with strawberry jam and complain to my mother that I never cooked. For their part my kids tell their kids that all I ever did was read books all day and never cooked.

I had no idea what to say. I agreed with him. Of course, I exaggerate the most in telling the kids the family mythology. Their proud great-grandparents who worked so hard. How tough their grandma once was, how she rode wild horses and jumped off cliffs into the lake and chased bears with a stick.

Yes, it's very true that whatever I tell or write, I warp and twist every story so it sounds better than it actually was when it happened. I can't stop myself. It's my job to dig into stories as I tell them. I don't just interrogate them, I want them to mean something, I want them to be something, I want them to be real, I want them to be great stories. I want to be proud of them. I want them to live.

Language is all about gesture in the moment—it is performance but performance that lasts because it is written down. Written language is gesture that has been frozen in time. It is therefore both a record and an illumination of history and art, and also potential for embarrassment.

As most writers discover, every story has an inner life that comes alive in the telling. There are an endless number of layers of this inner life—the storyteller can peel them back and back. A written story also has all these layers but the reader can only do the peeling if the storyteller leaves clues about the layers within the language itself and the images it makes.

In oral storytelling, the listeners are held captive, both by the skill of the storyteller and the intensity of the moment. To hear an oral story, you have to listen with concentration and believe in the story—hence the indignation of my grandson, who had listened to me since he was a baby, who believed me, and who had been betrayed when he was told that the stories I told him were "exaggerated."

How could I tell him that this shaping, this telling, this "exaggeration," this writing, was something I had spent a lifetime painfully learning to do—learning it in stolen moments in coffee shops while I was supposed to be doing laundry and in creative writing classes that I knew would never lead to a job or money. That I had spent years and years in agonized hours bent over a typewriter and then over a computer, trying to figure out how to be that thing, a writer, a real writer, a successful writer, a published writer. How to defend myself against a small boy who had just ripped the whole of my life apart with his scorn?

I don't actually exaggerate. I don't lie. I don't make things up. I shape stories in the best way I know how, in the clearest language I can use. They are all true, but a story comes alive in the making and in the form in which it is told.

It is one thing to say, "Your father used to go to his grandma's house in his pajamas in his bare feet." It is another thing to say, "When he was three or four, your father used to sneak out of bed before I was awake and run across the snowy yard in his bare bum with no shoes and go into Grandma's warm kitchen, where she would tuck him into her bed with warm quilts and make him hot chocolate with tiny pink marshmallows and toast with strawberry jam." Exactly.

But of course I exaggerate in the stories I tell my grandkids. Their parents did actually go to school. Sometimes, anyway. And the terrible stories of what they did as teenagers to my brand-new car are all true, mostly.

I couldn't defend myself against my beloved grandson so I didn't. I was revealed as a fake and a liar. But he was ten. I did try to point out to him, that, as a writer, I tried to tell interesting stories with meaning.

And he's in university now, having his own tussles with language so we have lots to talk about.

I have always had a sense of pride in being intensely honest, interrogating stories for meaning, reaching for understanding. When I did my doctoral thesis, I wrote a memoir and then I wrote about writing memoir, where I explore the issues of meaning, ethics, memory, language, context, history. Storytelling is a complex art and the language we use can be wonderful or treacherous.

And that's the thing; language is what we have, what makes the world, but words are so unreliable. Any writer must know what they mean and how they work, and why one word needs to go in a particular place and not another.

One of the most important things a fellow writer told me once was that "the ethics of language is in the aesthetics." I had to think about that for a long time until I understood it. I'm still thinking about it.

Language is endlessly complex, full of sound, rhythm, linkages between words, and cultural history. Language is a sensory movie; it contains smells, sounds, touch, sight, and taste. Good language is crunchy, you can almost taste it when you read. It has a satisfaction that is both pleasure and thought.

I hear it when I write it. And because the words must make a vivid movie, as well as vivid music, within the reader's head, the maxim is that such writing should be original, should show the reader a new way of writing an image, an idea, a character. The language needs to get the reader's attention but not so much as to jolt them out of the story. It's a fine balance but a necessary one.

Francine Prose, one of my favourite writers on this subject, in her book *Reading Like a Writer*, says this:

> Words to a writer are tools like colours to a painter. Writing depends on choosing one word over another and asking what each word is conveying. Close reading brings awareness to the words, and puts us inside the scene. We learn to write from within the scene and choose exact words to depict it.

So the form of how you write will always shape the meaning of the content. Form and content are inextricably linked. Because the meaning of writing is always in the context, and because often the meaning of the text is held within the images in the language, all the necessary information for the reader is contained only within the text and within the shape of that text.

And yet people go on talking with such faith, as if words meant something, as if language had some kind of actual real magic, as if chanting, singing, talking, describing, story-ing, would truly bring a new world into being for them. From whence could possibly come such touching and naive faith, the basis for all religion and public ritual, for politics and ritual and speech making and rhetoric of all kinds?

Once I believed in words as well. Once I thought stories, the truth of stories, only had to be revealed for the world to be changed. Once such a thing was true; once the personal was political and stories changed the world, but the world moved on and somehow, now, stories are still powerful but propaganda and sentiment and advertising have discovered the power of story and twisted it into unrecognizable forms.

Yes, a good true story can still change the world somewhat. The problem is, as I have grown older, many words, for me at least, have grown tired and so as words have become tired, so are the ways we tell stories. Especially stories about changing the world or making things better. Especially words about hope. Especially words that have become twisted and coded until their meanings are looped around each other like computer wires left too long in a case.

There are far too many such words right now; they are everywhere, infesting the internet and being used in all kinds of weird ways for which they were never intended, so many being over-used. Words like patriot, nationalist, globalism. Words like truth, freedom, liberation. Words like anger, oppression, safe, assault. Their meanings inverted, used in bizarre ways.

We are bombarded by such words now. There are few places to which to escape. In part because of social media, such words crawl everywhere, like lice. Often such words have become a code for groups. Just as the words, nationalist, globalist, and free speech have become weirdly turned on their heads. How does anyone know, now, what they mean?

Recently, I went to a literary reading which included spoken word poetry. An intense young woman took the stage. "Life," she said. And then again and again, after each line. "Life." Try as I could, I didn't understand the poem.

I have known since I was six and learned to read that words are my toys, my beloveds, my medium. I also have learned after years of writing and editing how slippery and layered words are; they come with such history, with so much overlaid onto them. A writer is a bit like a flycatcher; catch a word, pin it down and make it mean just what you want it to mean. You never quite can. Nor do you have any control over who the reader is, how she or he reads, how well or how badly.

I never knew how badly people read until I started reading online and then read the comments that people left under articles. Judging by these comments, many people could barely read or didn't understand how language worked or what words actually meant as opposed to what these readers wanted them to mean and assumed them to mean.

Still people have a deep faith in writing. I do as well, although that faith often trembles on a knife edge. I mentor lots of people who have good stories to tell and have no idea how hard writing is or how the meaning of a story will change within the writing of it, how it will surprise them. When I mentor new writers, I always tell them they won't really know what their book is about until they finish it. People are inevitably surprised by that. I am often surprised myself. But when a person at a reading asked me what I had learned from writing my most recent book, I said, "Every book teaches me to write that book." Which is true. And every book teaches me something about myself, but I am never quite sure what that is until I finish the book.

When the internet came along, of course one of the immediate reactions was that it would kill books. It has done the opposite. Somehow, people failed to notice that the internet is made of words (and yes, sigh, emojis). It might have something to do with the times and the increasing sense of powerlessness. A campaign on Facebook to achieve something can be immediate: to shame someone who has messed up, said something stupid, harmed an animal, left some garbage in a campsite.

But a campaign to stop global warming, change financial inequality, start a genuine political revolution seems to have no effectiveness on Facebook. In fact, there are always calls to keep Facebook "positive," and somehow this means to keep politics off it. It also in some undetermined way, seems to make people meaner and madder than ever. I have no idea why.

Perhaps every generation tells stories in its own way. Perhaps every generation formulates its grounding myths and those become a deep influence for how stories are now. Right now, we seem to be determined to tell stories that are barely language-based at all, that stretch language thin, that make it into gossamer bubbles that promise much and hold little weight.

Nevertheless, people go on having faith in language in some very odd ways and places—more faith than ever perhaps. In politics, in public, on social media, at funerals, at weddings, wherever they have a chance, people take the opportunity to make speeches, speeches full of rhetoric that promise much. Speeches that promise change and memory and better futures and great things to come; or on the other side, gloomy apocalyptic predictions, where no one seems to notice whether or not they happen.

As global climate change looms, as a growing variety of scenarios loom, people hold on to words as talismans, clutching them, wringing meaning and hope from them like wringing scrub water from a rag—this word, this word, this word, will save us. If only we can get the name right.

I am never having a funeral. It's impossible for anyone there to say anything true.

Lately I have been spending a lot of my time helping aging people write memoirs. Sometimes I get paid for this, which is one reason I do it. Sometimes, it forces me to rethink my life far too much. Rethinking my life, along with being in chronic pain is not a good combination—after all, I have made my mistakes and can't undo them and there is too much temptation to connect the pain with the many, many mistakes and see it as punishment—far too much temptation to withdraw into depression and solitude, but I've been there before and I'm not going back.

It takes energy to connect with people, although I love doing it. And there are also days when the energy I give to others allows pain to suck me into its suffocating coils. And the deeper I go, the less I can open myself to call for help, the less energy I have to say anything to people, the less I believe that anyone will believe what I say. Words fail me daily. Stories fail me. Instead, they circle me, buzzing me the way flies circle the horses. I have no defence against my own stories. Even writing them down feels chancy.

It instigates many more thoughts, too many stories and too many interpretations of my difficult crazy life. A story is not just words, it is also a multi-faceted mirror reflecting multiple truths, interpreting the world. So a story about my life right now is inevitably a story about pain and depression and, therefore, nothing more than a complaint, not a story at all. Here I am exaggerating again. Of course there are multiple stories about my life that are not sad complaints at all. Some days I write them down and they come out lucid and lucent like a glass bowl, all sparkle and light. And some I can remember, and I wonder if I have simply interpreted my life all wrong. And really, how would I know?

A memoir is never a failed story because a memoir is only an artifact, complete in itself. Words make it happen, words make it go around. Where words fail is when people wish them into closing the gap between reality and desire—when they want so desperately for words to bring true worlds into being. But words are only constructs that describe what we think of as a shared reality. But reality is made of things done, things enacted. Words are images with power that can easily go wrong.

Hitler built Nazi Germany with lots of words and then with brownshirts and with real weapons, real murders, real armies, real trains, and real death. Stalin made many speeches and made lots of deaths happen. Wars become an endless parade of stories. Some are told. Most are not. World War II is still a huge reservoir of stories because it changed everyone's life. No one escaped that war unscathed.

And no one who came through it came through without a story of some kind that could barely describe the reality of what had been done to them or what they had done to others. The whole of Europe was destroyed and then rebuilt. It was nothing but action—trains going everywhere carrying bodies full of words without stories attached to them because the stories had yet to be written. Most of them had no ending. Some of them still have no endings; perhaps now, as the generation that lived through the war disappears, they never will. Not all stories have meaning, not all stories have endings—death is not the end of a story—it is only the end of a life. It is the end of a certain source of words.

Language can and will fail to keep that person alive, to keep that person in memory, and that is our biggest hope and language's deepest failure. We believe so much that we can describe a life, a person, a wholeness, the reality of a person, in language, and it fails us so often. Instead, we have a shadow person, stories of a person, reflections, scattered bits of light, sun on water and rocks that fades through time and history. And an endless challenge to biographers, and historians, should they exist and be interested.

Now that I have reached a time in my life when I want and need to have deep conversations about aging, about identity shift, about dying, language is failing me again. I want to talk about dying and death, why I am here or not here, what to do and how to live and how to die. Some days I don't want to be alive. That is different than wanting to be dead but it's a fine distinction that most people can't or won't make. Aging is complex and difficult. It calls for horrible decisions at a time when decision making has gotten harder. My energy level is too low to cope with big changes and yet that is exactly what aging requires—moving and change.

I was standing at a party and a woman said to me with real tragedy in her eyes, "I have decided I have to get rid of my library."

"Yes, I did that," I said. "It was a big relief and now I keep buying books and then I give them away." Which I do. This led to a general discussion about getting rid of "stuff." It is hard enough to acquire but even harder to get rid of. I long for a bare house, just as I long for a simple life, without things like hope or a future cluttering it up.

I go to meditation, which the teacher says is thinking about not thinking. Perhaps what I want now is a story that is not-story. I want to play out on the edges and limits of language, to talk about not-being and not-meaning and the white space between and among all the words. But language, just when I need it most, fails me. Why have I spent all these years practising writing, so that now, when I think I might want to practise leaving writing, perhaps by talking and writing slowly about it instead, it so often leaves me alone and lonely, in a white cold silent room? I don't think I could stop writing. But some days, I would like it to be a little less insistent.

THE NAMES FOR DREAMS

I see the lake every day and the lake sees me. Or I pretend the lake sees me. I want to eat you, says the lake, or so I imagine. *Gobble gobble, glug glug*, whisper the pretty waves, the tinkly bits of ice in winter, the sheen of the black-blue-green depths that remain, even in summer, icy cold.

The lake does eat careless people, people who go out in boats when it is too stormy, people who think they can canoe in the wind. The lake ate the homesteader who built our farm. He went out fishing in his canoe in the spring and never came home.

When I was a child, I would get down off the ancient smelly school bus, change my clothes, do my farm chores and go to the lake. Sometimes the rocks beside the lake hummed and sang in the shimmering late afternoon sun. As the reflections flickered and danced over the rocks, they sang soft, sighing harmonies.

One day, I mentioned this to my mother. I said how wonderful it was. She looked puzzled and the next day she came with me to the beach. She heard it, I'm sure of it, but she still looked puzzled and then she dismissed it. "It's just insects in the rocks," she said. And the next time I went to the lake, the rocks were silent. I accepted that I had done something wrong, but I didn't know what it was.

But really, ancient lake that has been my playground all my life, and is now my grandchildren's playground, you say nothing, you have no stories, except the occasional rumours of monsters, of giants, of leaping sturgeons.

THE WHITE ROOM —129

Kootenay Lake is bounded by the Purcell and Selkirk Mountain ranges on the east and west respectively. The lake occupies a long deep valley known as the Purcell Trench, which probably formed about 70–100 million years ago during the uplift of the Selkirk Mountains and the emplacement of masses of granite. It is likely that the major fault now followed by the Lower Kootenay River also formed around this time.

The Kootenay Region was extensively glaciated during the Pleistocene epoch of the last few million years. Final deglaciation began about 15,000 years ago.

Higher elevations became ice-free first, while melting ice blocks lingered at some places in the valley bottoms. Ice and glacial drift dammed the general westward drainage, producing Glacial Lake Kootenai (now Kootenay Lake), which at first drained southward. Over the next 10,000 years or so, the level of Kootenay Lake declined further through a series of stages. After having its head near present-day Bonners Ferry for thousands of years, the non-freshet level of Kootenay Lake lowered again around 2500 years ago to the natural level recorded historically (about 530 metres above sea level). This most recent lake stand was subsequently held by the bedrock outcrops on the Lower Kootenay River, which had become a series of large waterfalls as the river removed sediment from them.

When the ice melted, the fish began to return, salmon swimming up from the ocean, investigating new habitats. However, salmon never made it into Kootenay Lake because they couldn't get above Bonnington Falls, below Nelson. The salmon who had come up into the lake before the lake lowered enough for the falls to emerge, stayed in the lake and became our iconic Kokanee, or redfish, which are indigenous to the Columbia River as well as Kootenay Lake.

As the lake level fell, sediments were deposited alongside the ice farther north as the melting glacial lobe shrank from the mountain slopes bounding the Purcell Trench, gradually uncovering the top of the Porthill Bench, upon which the town of Creston is now situated. After a long time, the outlet shifted northward to the present west arm of Kootenay Lake, where the river flows south and joins the Columbia River at Castlegar.

There are so many other stories I can tell of you, old lake. But they are my stories, not mythic stories. The Ktunaxa Indigenous people have many stories of the lake, and the monster that once dwelt within it. In some places, the smooth granite lake rocks have pictographs, but the Ktunaxa don't talk about them. Nor do they want people to know where they are. Several of the more obvious ones have been defaced with graffiti.

So, what do I know about this lake besides its history and my own stories? My Irish friend, Sharon Blackie, who teaches Irish mythology, writes:

> ...the idea of an Otherworld (or several) which runs alongside this one, which in some sense can be reached from this one, which influences this one, and which has characteristics of the *mundus imaginalis*, is a key aspect of shamanic cosmologies throughout the world.

Yes, in Ireland, every pond seems to have a story—in Scotland every bog a mystery. Kootenay Lake and the Columbia River do indeed have many other Ktunaxa First Nation stories, but the Ktunaxa are a close and careful people who keep their stories alive among themselves.

We, the settlers, the invaders, the colonialists, the whities, whatever names we have earned or deserve, we who live beside this giant lake and these mountains and these scarred and mined and roaded hills that we have managed to run over in every possible direction—we have no stories at all except those of our brief and recent history of pioneers—and even those we succeed in forgetting almost as soon as those pioneers have died. My father and my grandfather's stories of our farm were about fighting with the land, with clearing trees, with directing water where they needed it to go, and of killing predators and other wild animals so their farmland would be safe.

Within a generation or two, the land that the people homesteaded—built houses, planted gardens and orchards on—was usually subdivided and sold off, the houses bought, renovated, sold, renovated again, and so even these pioneer stories disappear too fast.

We in North America are good at losing the past. Since industrialization, the supreme story of North America has been of individual change, movement, growth, where no one put down roots anywhere because there was always somewhere else to go.

Thus, we in North America are a people with almost no stories, no mythology. Our ancestors, who were indigenous somewhere once, left behind almost all their stories and songs. Now we, the descendants of these newcomers, live in this gap and believe it has always been so, that we have no stories and no history, only a constant newly created present time. The stories of our ancestors are gone, left in the "old country."

When my ancestors came here, Canada was a new "empty" country where everything would be made new. The government told them, "It's free land if you can claim it."

And so they did. A wild country made new in the visions of its settler pioneer discoverers who believed with deep and profound sincerity that they were building the future. And so they were and so they did, with deep sincerity and profound ignorance and harsh work and early death and many accidents. And much hope at the prospect of what they were creating. Everything new: a new land, a new civilization, a new prosperity, a new country, a new future. New was the word. Old was forgotten and left behind.

But Sharon Blackie also says:

> A surprising proportion of people who take my courses are from North America—more than half. I'm always struck by the deep need that so many people have to find an authentic way to weave their ancestral heritage into their daily lives in the very different countries where they now live. It's clear to me that a lack of this heritage leaves an enormous hole in their lives.

As I drive home to my farm, the pounding November rain and wind rips the last shreds of leaves off the maple trees. I pass by miles of dead orchards and old homesteads. I live in a valley of lost dreams. I pass the farm just five miles south of where I live now, the farm my grandfather bought for my parents as a wedding present, now empty again; I pass old homesteads; I pass the homesteads that Italian immigrant families terraced, the mountainside ribbed with long stone walls in imitation of their village in Italy. It is certainly not for lack of work and effort and sweat that people no longer farm in this valley or that the children have gone elsewhere. Some farmers who still grow grain or who export hay to China are making money. The day may come when local organic farming will again support this valley.

Where I live, people are mostly gone now during the winter, gone to Mexico or Arizona. Gone to Calgary where they really live. They build huge monstrous houses here that they never live in. They come in the summer, they are here for the view. They have locked up most of the lakeshore and seem bewildered by the number of animals that take up residence in and around and under their houses when they are away three seasons of the year.

They fight back, good middle-class folks, sealing off their attics from bats, putting up bat houses, sealing their basements from weasels and mice, their log walls from flies, their gardens from deer. They fight back hard against this place they love so much.

They go on colonizing. They make neat, gravelled paths through the trees. They plant flowers and mow lawns and cut brush and weed whack under trees and pour herbicide on anything that isn't grass. They work hard almost all the time they are here, their machines running and ready. They are amazing in their determination to continue the colonizing of the countryside even though the pioneers' steely-eyed determination to found a new country and a new civilization is long gone. These Calgary pioneers merely want to beat back the grass and trees and weeds and the animals long enough to have a little space for their grandkids. Good luck. Nature is resilient. Nature will eat you. Will eat us.

North America now mostly looks tame and full of cities and cars, but underneath the land is wild and restless and full of power. Kootenay Lake surges in its narrow rocky canyon, fragile and powerful both, stopped with dams, and penned and temporarily under control. For now.

The lake road I drive every day is sidelined with houses on every estuary. And every creek has washed out at least once in my lifetime.

Nothing is under control.

It was in a discussion with a friend that I first identified the gap in my life that I hadn't known was there, but which had been hurting and bothering me all my life, rather like having pain I was born with and thus couldn't identify. She was talking with some enthusiasm about a writer who was attempting to blend Celtic stories with First Nations stories to create something new and how wonderful she found this.

I read the blog and found this mix unsatisfying and irritating and wondered why. As usual, I went for a walk, trying to figure it out. I went to the lake and the fields and for the first time in my life. I noticed that they were empty of stories and empty of voices.

As they had always been. The stories I had made of them were my stories. The stories of the farm and the lake and the mountains and the creeks where I have lived for seventy years are my family stories. We were a small clan and our stories will die with us except for the few I have written down and the few that my grandchildren will remember. When the farm is sold, even those stories will disappear. There are no myths here and no one is interested in the old stories. They are not really that old and not really that interesting. There are my mother's ghost stories, which get a little more exaggerated whenever I tell them, and the story of Pete's lost gold, which may someday take on the aura of a myth. And the lake monster. And the places we knew together as children, the Hog Pasture, the Main Beach, Bone Bay, Sawdust Bay. As children, we named every place on the farm and every place had a story from which we derived that name. Those names will end with me.

Now I make stories out of the farm, out of ghosts, out of animals, out of neighbours, out of children, out of the people who come and go in my life. All of them lifted, transformed into stories, light as air, drifting away like music, shining, like the smoke of the fire before me, drifting as my memories will drift eventually, into the gaps and clumps and frozen neurons of my brain and disappear.

The stories and myths that North Americans live with are primarily European with an occasional sentimental, sloppy sideways paean to some partially understood Indigenous idea—Coyote or Raven as Trickster, Salmon as this ideal of return and fertility and so on. But mostly, what we have are European myths and fairy tales reinterpreted for mass audiences through mass media. These myths are reinterpreted according to current tastes and so they flex and move oddly, and usually become sentimentally heroic.

Our myths and fairy tales are still primarily those that came out of the ancient forests of Europe. "Woods have always been a place of in betweenness, somewhere one might slip from one world to another," says Robert Macfarlane.

But in North America, the forest was both a resource and an enemy. We are still cutting it down, spraying it with Roundup, turning it into money.

We are very slowly rewriting our ideas for forests. But "nature" stories, in North America, are still, far too often, colonial stories, where the forest is either sentimental and beautiful, or savage and dangerous. Not much in between.

For a long time, I did search, along with many others, for a genuine sense of ritual and mythology that would connect me here, connect me into First Nations ritual, into the land. I did work for a First Nations college for several years and went to ceremonies and sweats, always an outsider.

After I left there, I went to a sweat with only white women, a promising event on the flyer, but not much in reality. The women participating complained it was too hot, too dark, too sweaty. They crawled out, they left, one woman cried and then fainted outside on the beach. An immediate crisis and all the attention was on her. When she was well and sitting up and the sweat was forgotten, I left.

I tried other places, other circles, other meetings, other discussions, along with many other people, also searching. I took my mother to church. I loved church. People accepted my non-Christian presence, and every week I wondered at the language and its odd meanings even as its rhythms and deep bass cadences invaded my poetry. But the language itself seemed almost silly, mostly begging an imaginary god for a non-existent mercy. I had no idea what I was doing there, apart from taking my mother to sing in the choir.

But none of it took. None of it was comfortable. None of the rituals, women's circles, sweats, Wicca, meditations, chanting and handholding sessions were places I could stay in. My place was and is the mountains, the trees, the lake, the ravens, the squirrels calling, all the things that have shaped my life. My place was and is the soil and the fruit trees and the plants and the dogs running and the horse snuffling my pockets for apples. Those are my rituals.

And so I walk a land with only my own stories to tell to the trees and the lake. *Gobble gobble*, says the lake. Root and grow, say the trees. I can be content with this, almost. I can wander down to the beach with the dogs and a cat and perhaps even a couple of horses and sit on the same rocks with their goblin ancient faces and never feel alone. Perhaps the stories here are just so much bigger and older than I can ever know, and the only sane and profoundly animal-human connection I can have is to accept that this is all I know for now.

The stories are there. Will they wait for us to hear them? What will it take? Where do stories come from? It's a mystery. Do they come from the trees, the rocks whispering in the sun in the late afternoon, the lake river curling into the cold arms of the lake? Is it only people who tell stories?

When the winds have names and each place name has a story, will we begin to root our lost selves into this land?

Sharon Blackie writes:

> If you're in America or Canada, then no matter how challenging the history of settlement might be, you're part of the stories of that land now, too. The stories of the land are always growing and transforming. They are the bridges.

I listen and watch. The bridges are there. I put them there as a child. I just have to find them again.

As a child, like most children, I lived intensely in an imaginary world. Sticks turned into horses, the logs at the beach into spaceships, a flat clearing in the trees above the lake became a palace. I took it for granted that my imaginary landscape would be whatever I wanted it to be that day and it always was, until one day, it vanished.

I had read a book about a boy who trained an elephant and became its "mahout." I loved horses and now I also wanted an elephant. Fortunately, just below our farmhouse, in a small valley with a creek, was a large rock that was just the right shape to be an elephant. I clambered onto its head with a long stick and off we went through the jungle.

Until the day when I climbed up, sat down, and all was quiet. The rock was still a rock. The jungle had vanished. The stick in my hand was a piece of wood. It was like waking up from a flying dream, and knowing I could fly if I just remembered the trick. I sat there a while, not believing that the world of magic had vanished so utterly, so fast.

I kept bits of it. I could, and still do, put myself to sleep at night by dreaming of riding, or dreaming of an imaginary realm where anything could happen.

But I have kept looking for it. Something in me has carried that loss. Something in me searches, always for the story that I once knew was there.

All my life, I have been a walker. Now my heart won't let me walk much, and the magic places on the mountains are closed to me. But when I was young, even after the imaginary world closed its doors, I still knew that places on the mountains or on the lakeshore contained some kind of magic.

One day I had a conversation with a First Nations elder. I asked him about the pictographs on the rocks near our farm. He said, "Oh, that is where our young people would go and talk to spirits."

The next chance I got, I went to that place, sat on the rocks, lonely, and waited. And waited.

Nothing shifted, it was the lake, my lake that I had known all my life, the sheer granite point jutting out into deep black-green water, with the pictographs on its smooth slab sides.

And then one day, much later, I was walking there, going up the hill. I stopped to look at a stand of enormous ponderosa pine trees that had somehow escaped being logged; they shone red in the afternoon sun, and as I stood there, I saw them see me back. "Don't come here," they said, because my immediate impulse had been to walk among them. "You killed us," they said. I stood there, stopped, and wondered how to be among them again in a good way.

The problem with a psychic experience like this is that it is both true and untrue, and there is no way of knowing and no way of choosing. I saw the trees. They saw me back. Current research by great scientists like Suzanne Simard and Merlin Sheldrake would seem to back up my perception of the trees, in some way, "seeing." That land has been logged at least twice—when I was a kid it was a tangle of downed trees and skid trails made by the logging horses, but these trees grew in an isolated cleft in the cliff.

As these ponderosa pine trees glowed bright scarlet, I had looked hard at them, noticing. The trees were big, not massive, but much bigger than the forest around them. I had never noticed this grove before. It was set off to one side of the road in a deep gully. People have bought the land and made a new road. So perhaps I had never actually seen them before. In human terms, it was a scene of momentary intense beauty. It didn't need interpreting, just that I noticed and acknowledged that it was there.

But I stood locked there by such noticing. I heard the tree voices as hostile and unwelcoming. In their history, humans were destructive. Humans are predators of trees. If we all knew that trees knew we were killing them, we might see them differently. Scientists and writers like Suzanne Simard and Merlin Sheldrake and many others are showing us the way.

Perhaps what we have really lost are the pathways in our brains that would let us believe that such an experience is real. I have always been puzzled by First Nations stories, puzzled equally, by anthropologists' interpretations of such stories, which never seem to explain much. One day I listened to Jeanette Armstrong, a Knowledge Keeper for the Okanagan Nation, exclaim angrily that animals and plants were not totems to First Nations. They were and are teachers.

And I began to imagine, what would it be like to live in a world where humans had no sense of superiority to animals, if in fact, animals seemed faster, stronger and often wiser. With mysterious abilities and languages. And if, in fact, you grew up knowing and having relationships with animals on a basis of shared respect and knowledge, how differently would you see them?

Perhaps it's not possible to unthink myself out my own settler culture. Perhaps I can only wander the edges of another imagined world. Perhaps it is enough, for now, to allow the imagining, the wondering, the mystery, and to listen for the stories that will come one day, when people are ready to hear and know them.

Aging has helped so much with this, allowed me more separation from ambition. It has steadily decolonized my mind from what I thought I knew. One of the great, seldom-recognized gifts of age and disability is the understanding of how little I know, how big my questions still are. It has allowed me the grace of slow pondering walks with the white cat where I marvel at the light, marvel at how grass shines with energy, stop to look at ants and white butterflies, and stand still for long periods just to listen.

Sharon Blackie says:

> The guiding mythology of western culture is not only intensely heroic and individualistic in nature, it is also profoundly goal-oriented. What might a post-heroic mythology look like instead? What stories would we tell if we thought that living a good and meaningful life had nothing to do with finding treasure, defeating our enemies, or living happily ever after, but was about learning to live more deeply, day by day, in a challenged and constantly challenging world? What stories might we find which offer us a richer set of values to live by?

Which show us that being and becoming are
just as important as achieving and doing?

It is likely that mythology is built from something that
happened, that grew and regrew over time and with retelling.
The Ktunaxa Creation story in the Kootenays is about a
monster in Kootenay Lake and in the river. I've seen the lake
monster twice. The first time I was with my grandson. Just
at dusk, as we were getting ready to leave the beach, far out,
a huge sturgeon flew up, out of the middle of the wide, flat,
dark lake, twisted around, and dropped back with a mighty
crash. It screamed as it did so.

And I have seen the bony white backs of sturgeon min-
gled, once, as they moved down the lake in a group. Sturgeon
are bottom feeders and are rarely seen. And almost never together.

And when I was a child, I knew two people, both completely sombre truth tellers, who had also seen the monster.
One was the schoolteacher from our local one-room school.
The other was Wally Johnson, the trapper whose whole live-
lihood depended on knowing about animals and their habits.

So we have facts as well as history and imagination and
stories, which seem, at some point, to coalesce and condense
into something we call mythology: the Greek stories of naiads
and fauns, the Celtic story of the Green Man, the Sidhe story
of the Wild Hunt; and the Nordic stories—my favourites with
their horses, swords and big drunken parties. And so many
others.

And in North America? Perhaps it takes much, much longer
for myths to appear. Perhaps it takes time and knowledge and
a people who are entangled with, and deeply knowledgeable
about, where they live. Right now, we have settler mythology and a bizarre mixture of settler myths: stories of racism,

of pride, of endurance, of powerful men, of lone heroes, of "taming" the land and its inhabitants. Of strong individuals building communities and civilization, of power and profit and greed and struggle and many people being hurt and many people succeeding in their dreams. Settler myths all have a bit of an unearthly glow over them, always somewhat bigger in the re-telling than perhaps the reality was. I have my own family mythology of heroes and outlaws and brave pioneer great-grandfathers and great-uncles and horse-riding intrepid great-grandmothers. Such stories are easily lost, mislaid, misjudged, retold. I tell all of my writing students now to write memoir because stories disappear so easily. History disappears or is twisted and retold to serve someone else's purpose. Some believe me and every month now, we meet and work on these stories of our lives. This is only a small gift I can give the land and its history.

I stand up, shut the computer, call the dogs and the white cat, wander the road to the lake, see what it's up to now, perhaps take a photograph of the clouds and light show that goes on over the mountains, a constant, endlessly changing and shifting story of colour and light for those who see it. Perhaps it's a new poem, a new photo, a new essay. Perhaps it's this one.

But I wait for it. I wait for the singing. I heard it once. It's still there. I just have to wait.

MUSIC AND MY MOTHER

My mother always had a grief in her that I could not reach. I spent much of my childhood trying to make this up to her. I tried to carry her grief for her. In the spring, I brought her the first dandelion blooms. I would coax and coax her to come out for a swim with us, her children. She was always too busy, she said, but occasionally she came. It was always an event. She wore a bathing cap to protect her hair, which she put up in pin curls every morning. She would wade slowly into the water, protesting that it was too cold. We ran in and out to show her how wonderful it was. She would sit on the beach in the sun for a few minutes and then hurry home.

On Mother's Day, I would hustle about in the kitchen, self-importantly making her breakfast. I would put flowers on a tray and carry it upstairs to her room. But nothing I did ever really reached that grief. It took me a long time to understand what she carried, and why.

It wasn't just my mother; all the women whose children I went to school with had been women who, during the war, had worked, had gotten jobs, had contributed to the war effort. And after the war, they were all laid off; they got married, they had children. They never divorced. It was all they were allowed to do. Most of them didn't have driving licences or bank accounts or training for any particular job, so if they left a bad marriage, they would be adrift and helpless in the world.

When I was very young, we had a small record player in a red box on top of the black bookcase under the window in the living room. There was always music pouring out of it. Then we got a bigger record player, a "stereo," because even when she could barely afford shoes for her children, my mother managed to afford opera records, and all day long, arias filled our farmhouse, and my mother's clear soprano rang from the kitchen as she cooked and cleaned.

My mother had dropped out of school when she was twelve because her mother, my grandmother, had cancer. My mother had to cook for a boarding house full of men, which was how my grandmother made a living. Her husband, Fred, was often not working. But my grandmother miraculously survived the cancer, and my mother went on working in the boarding house.

But then, when the war began, my mother was full of hope for a new life. She was eighteen, she moved to Vancouver and lived with her aunt Daisy, her father's sister, and her uncle, Murdoch McLeod, a travelling optometrist, and their seven kids. She got a job at Boeing Aircraft Factory and worked carrying rivets from the machines to the riveters inside the airplanes. She took singing lessons along with her brother, Charlie. They both had fine operatic voices. Aunt Daisy played the piano and her various cousins sang and played violin and piano.

When the war ended, her singing teacher encouraged her to go to Toronto and enroll in music school. She came home to her family, ostensibly to borrow the money to go to Toronto, and married our father instead. She gave various reasons for this: her singing teacher was lecherous, her grandfather, who was wealthy, wouldn't loan her the money, she had stage fright and couldn't sing on stage. It was probably a combination of all three. But we all knew the undercurrent of sadness in her life, and that music, not us, not our father, was her first love.

How had she come to music? Her parents were poor; her father, Fred Klingensmith, was often away working as a saw filer in Nakusp. He was also an itinerant prospector, which made it hard for him to keep a job. Eventually, he moved out.

To be a single woman in Creston at that time was shameful—so shameful that when my grandmother began seeing another man, she was threatened with excommunication by the Anglican bishop.

After my mother and father moved to our farm, when I was five years old, my mother joined the Metropolitan Opera Society and ordered opera records through the mail. They came every month. CBC Radio broadcast Metropolitan Opera on Saturday afternoons and nothing interfered with her listening to this. We all listened.

Opera records were a luxury. We ate well on the farm but my parents rarely had any extra money. Our mother scrounged a little egg and milk money and it went to opera records. My father didn't complain about this, oddly enough, although he complained about everything else.

So my mother collected tenors the way other people might collect rock stars. She fell in love with Jussi Björling, and Mario Lanza and Enrico Caruso, Paul Robeson, and many others. She told us their sad stories, and they were mostly sad or at least she made them so.

My mother had tiny delicate hands. She did up her hair every morning with bobby pins and then combed it out just before lunch. She wore lipstick every day. She was hospitable and sweet when people came to visit and then she made fun of them when they left.

She said often that she hated society and loved living

away from what she saw as the hypocrisy of people. She loved having children and our father did not. He had never wanted children. But she was proud of us, her children, and proud of our independence and afraid for us in equal measure. Our father saw us as free labour when he could corral us long enough to put us to work.

She was often ill and music was her main comfort and escape from pain. When we were young we lived in a mining camp; the houses were mostly unfinished and damp and my mother developed rheumatic fever and an enlarged heart. When we moved to the farm, the workload was unrelenting. We had two milk cows, so she had to have the milk strainers and separators sterilized and ready when my father brought the milk in at 6:00 a.m. She made butter and cheese, which my father sold, and every day, one of us was sent to collect the eggs from the dusty chicken pen. Then the eggs had to "candled," held in front of a light in the basement, at night. This was to ensure they didn't have cracks or blood spots in the yolks.

My parents tried every way possible to make money off the farm, and every one of them eventually failed. One year I helped my mother clean and freeze three hundred chickens because they had gotten an illness and had to be killed. We ate chicken every night that winter. My mother canned hundreds of jars of fruit and vegetables every fall. She made three full meals every day. She baked every day.

Every holiday—Christmas, Easter, New Year's, Thanksgiving—she cooked enormous meals and we all came, her adult children, even if we weren't speaking to each other, which was often the case. She did all of it, often in pain.

In her fifties, she developed a form of arthritis in her hands. Her hands were red and swollen and she couldn't touch anything. Since she had to go on baking, making butter, cleaning chickens, peeling and canning fruit, she worked in agony. She cured this one through prayer somehow. She knelt down in sheer desperation one day and prayed to Jesus to take the pain from her hands. Whatever happened, it worked. She told us about it with some wonder.

She always had a bad heart from rheumatic fever and bad circulation, and when she got older, she developed painful leg ulcers that wouldn't heal, so she wore pressure stockings that were difficult to put on. She had to roll them up, then unroll them inch-by-tight-inch and fasten them to a girdle.

And still she sang. When we were in the kitchen cooking together, we sang together as well.

Then very abruptly, she stopped. Someone had criticized her singing. She would never say who it was or what they had said. "My voice is gone," she told me.

I went away from my mother for many years. I went off to work and go to university. And then I came back to the farm to write because I had enough money to survive on for a year with a part-time job teaching and some grant money. She may have stopped singing at home, but she still sang in the church choir. I went with her the last ten years, driving her because she couldn't drive on her own. I loved going to the little country church and to the tea afterwards, with everyone fussing a bit over their latest operation or their heart or what the damn doctor had said now or what the drugs did.

By this time, I had become a writer. I had gone through two marriages and my kids were grown. I had been through my own battles. I had worked as a radical activist, a feminist, an environmentalist; I had marched with many signs, worked in the women's movement, the peace movement, and at a First Nations college. Much of this experience was bitter. People betrayed each other in incremental ways despite high ideals and utopian language. I was exhausted. Every morning, I went to my mother's house for coffee and every afternoon, we went for a walk together, and when I wasn't teaching or driving my mother to town, I wrote and wrote.

One day my mother looked at me and said, "You were always such a happy child. What happened?"

Much later, as a result of the car accidents and the heart trouble, I was in a pain clinic in the hospital for a while. At this point my mother was dead. I was talking to the very kind psychiatrist who was trying to help me. We discovered a mutual interest in opera. After we talked, I went back to my hospital bed and called up on YouTube, Puccini's *La bohème* with soprano Victoria De Los Angeles and tenor Jussi Björling. I discovered—in fact was astonished to find—my mother, curled and joyous, inside the music, happy, singing.

When I was a child, I would sit beside the stereo, listening to opera or symphonies and my mother would say, "Listen for the stories inside the music. Listen for the pictures." And she was right. There were stories and pictures in music. She gave me a sense of beauty. A sense of meaning. A sense of how something as transitory as music can live forever, embody the past, wrap a human life into transcendence. Music is always in the present tense.

When I was twelve, I took the money I had saved from selling fruit on the farm fruit stand and bought a piano. I had a bunch of "teach yourself piano" books and every day, I worked my way through each consecutive piece in the books. I wanted piano lessons but there was no one to teach me and it cost far too much even if there had been a teacher.

I became a writer because I never had the opportunity to become a musician. But music came first and I discovered that music lives in writing as well—writing is music made with language. Now I listen for it as I once listened for my mother, her high soprano notes floating out over the farm, across the fields, all the way to the beach, calling us, her children, home.

ANOTHER COUNTRY

FRAGILE

I teeter forward on the beach with my iPad, (my balance never good now). I walk carefully, trying to catch a picture of my two dogs and my cat playing together. But it only takes one slip, a bit of ice under snow and I'm down. This time it isn't my body that shatters, but the glass on my iPad, a web of cracks that spreads across the screen. I pick it up, hold it to my chest like a wounded animal and then pick myself up, which takes a good while longer. The next day, my son covers the fragile face of the iPad with packing tape and it still works, well enough, for now.

I heard a simulacrum of myself described on the radio the other day—a "fragile" senior, someone with chronic illness, often made worse by the medical system, by the hurried impersonal attention of doctors and nurses, by lights, needles, drugs, machines, noise, and bad food. Why would anyone go there? Not I, says this little red hen. My father always said the hospital was where you went to die. He was right.

Some days, I am not so fragile. On the good days, I am robust, full of joy. My days are busy—full of work I love. I only notice my fragility when something comes up that throws me into turmoil. Usually something to do with money, or someone being vindictive, or someone in distress, someone who is angry. I never thought I would be someone who could settle for routine. Why would I? My life as an adult was a chaos of survival, whirling, always in some despair, never enough money or time for any of it, and still doing forty things at once. Kids and kids' friends and my friends and animals and the farm and writing, writing, writing—always, all of it needing more time and attention and money than I could ever spare. I never noticed chaos because I lived in the centre of it while things whirled around, or broke, or went away forever.

Now I am, at long last, weary and mostly happy for a quiet life and the same walk every day. Except, it's not quiet; there's the world, still wildly spinning, and the stars, tiny bits of infinity, poking through the night sky and bringing cold from outer space with them. There are the animals, with their mysterious lives, the plants and trees whispering to each other through root ends and mycelium. All quiet does is let in the big questions, the ones sleeping in the lake, hidden in the blue vastness of the Purcells. The ones I always knew were there.

I walk encumbered: a cell phone in one pocket, plus the broken iPad; the phone because my kids worry; the iPad so I can peer at the boles of trees, cracks within rocks, dens under stumps, at moss caught suddenly by light, at the light on the lake, the spangled clouds. I like using the iPad to frame things. I understand now how photographs "capture" things because I can bring them home and look at them again. In the same way that writing creates an artifact that in some way removes the writer from his or her own history, a photograph captures and changes the experience of a moment.

Light is the mystery. Each moment changes the light and shows me something I've never noticed before. All day, the weather shifts, the clouds move and make momentary patterns, but my time and my breath is limited. I pick the moment the world shows me and I miss the rest.

The fragility of moments, like the ripples that stir in the heart of the lake and gurgle nonsense to the one hesitating on the shore—the one who can't live and can't die, caught in some evanescent bubble that is lasting a bit too long.

I was always tough and glad to be tough. I believed there was a way out of every trap, if I fought hard enough, even if that involved smashing things. I never cried because it was a waste of time but cold quiet inner rage was always useful. Now as I walk among the new baby pine trees recolonizing what was once an orchard and a hayfield, I am conscious that I am old, and this land which I have cared for, for so long, must eventually be sold and probably quite violently turned into houses and "gardens" and septic fields, and lawns mowed weekly and covered with weedkiller.

Ecosystems weaken under the loads humans impose, and civilization itself has become fragile with too many overloaded systems, politics and ideas fragmenting. I read about it. It all seems connected, me as a fragile patient tied to a fragile place, a fragile elder, a fragile senior, a fragile human, living during chaotic times in the history of humanity.

Once I believed that the world was well. I believed in government and democracy. I hadn't realized yet that the governments of the world are run by human beings who are easily broken or bribed or confused. Once I thought I knew who I was, and what I was meant to do in the world, but aging destroys that in many people; not so far in me, but looking down the road, I see a final battle that I can't win. I like the idea of a medically chosen and induced death because it gives me some terms on which I can choose to leave—my own time, my own place. Death doesn't give us a lot of choices. That one, at least, can be mine.

But fragility is a cliché we all learn at different times and in different ways. A broken iPad, a broken car, a broken brain. And the iPad survived, as do I. Although often at night, I wish

I had not survived—not wanting to be dead, just not wanting to be in this world, like this. There's a big gap between not wanting to be in this world and being actively suicidal. Suicide is action; I may sometimes wish, wistfully and gently, to not wake up in the morning, but it is only a wish and when I do wake up, there is a conscious choice to swing my legs down, to stand up slowly and walk to the kitchen to pour out cat food and then make tea. The cat makes me get up. So do the dogs. If they weren't here, what would I do?

Things can seem tough until they are broken—a family breaks apart in slow increments, year after year, people peeling away, not answering messages, misunderstandings growing, family dinners petering out. Any relationship needs work but a family is a complex system and when one part slows or disappears, the rest disengage as well; family is an apparatus that melts, some pieces hang on, the rest grow smaller and smaller as pieces are swept away in a slow flood of funerals, disengagements, people moving, people growing up.

Now, realistically, most days, it's just me and the cat and the dog. What do I do now that my world is ineluctably broken and there is nothing more to be done—no new job or new school or new book or new relationship to break the suffocation, sweep the fragments from my mouth and nose and ears and rise up again? Nothing to rise up for, nothing to rise up with. Here is where existentialism really meets the hard road. There was always something to get up for—kids, jobs, school, animals, books and more books. Now there is only the cat, the bed, the stove, the house, all of which can and will be shed. How does anyone do this? How is aging so much loss? How do we bear this?

My old dog puffs her way up from the beach and when we both stop to rest, she stares at me from the darkest depths of her soul, fixing me with her almost black eyes, rimmed with white hairs, my seal dog, doggy mascara, to tell me she is going to leave soon. I hold her head, we will both be fine, I tell her, she just has to make it home, one more time, up the hill, in the house, food and bed and sleep. Comfort for me. Bit of chocolate, wine, sleep. What I have to live for, for now.

I am not broken, yet, only fragile. Only more conscious of fragility. How I miss my young child pride in being strong, lithe, fast. How well I remember because it saved me, every day, from people, from school, where their glances burned my skin, their voices shrill and harsh.

There was always that moment, when I stepped into the trees and then stopped, listened, a raven would ghost over-head, the barely heard whisper of its wings. Far off, a squirrel, and then another, as the forest woke up and the trees passed on the message. All that I know now, I knew then. Now I can make words for it. What I knew then was how to go, far and slow, and stop often to listen, through the many chambered rooms of the forest, each space different, different trees, different feeling, different rocks, some spaces welcoming, some threatening. I went into a space once where I didn't belong and a black shape leapt from the trees and flew away. I ran. But other spaces I squatted under the trees and breathed and listened. Once I made a hideout from branches, upon a high hill and then I could have a small fire and cook some food.

I think children naturally go feral very easily. In my case, I turned wild easily because no one told me not to. I learned it because no one was watching and no one seemed to notice I was gone. The forest and the mountains offered so much more than was offered to me in the house, where my mother was harried and busy—loving—but driven by the needs and demands of a farm and four young children and my father, who was also driven by the demands of feeding and clothing his family from what he could make off a small farm. Which he never quite could. So then he would work off the farm and come home and do the chores, essentially two long work days, and his children cowered from his needs and demands and threats they couldn't ever fulfill.

But outside in the forest all was cool silent peace and the promise of adventure.

And then there was the moment, coming home in the early winter dark—it never seemed to occur to anyone that a kid wandering in the woods in the dark might not be safe; it certainly never occurred to me when I would stand in the cold darkness in the yard and watch my family at the supper table. I usually wore cheap rubber boots on the farm, and they would be full of snow and my soaking wet socks would have slid into the toes of the boots. Often, snow was falling and often I would stick out my tongue and taste each fragile flake.

I knew I would go in. I knew I had to. But I was divided, liminal, neither wild nor tame, looking back at the woods from where I had come, from sitting under a tree, breathing and listening. To the house, where my family would be squabbling, where my father oversaw the dinner table, with archaic rules we didn't understand: no elbows on the table, no whistling, no slouching; and where he either lectured us or teased us or made us do math. My mother's food was always stupendously good, and I was cold and hungry. But going in was always hard, like pushing through a wall of pulsating light and noise that hit my eyes and ears like a series of blows. The way to do it was to get in, sit down, shovel food into my face, and get to my room fast with the excuse of homework. But of course, that didn't work either. I had to help clear the table, help do the dishes, help because I was a girl, help because I was willing to help and my younger sister would dissolve into tantrums instead of helping, so my mother had given up asking her to do much of anything.

And then the escape, finally, to my own room, where I would lean on the windowsill and stare at the white peaked mountains, so perfect, so far away because that was where I belonged, where I should be and where it would be utterly peaceful. Nostalgic for a place I had never been and would never go. I didn't know then how fragile that moment outside was, a bubble trapped briefly between, where I couldn't stay and would always miss.

So then bed and books. Always, with such relief, books. The classic story of reading under my blankets with a flashlight and being caught by my mother. But still I read and read.

I also didn't know that this divide would follow me all my life, that my father's anger would follow me through my life, that no matter what I did or how hard I tried, it would never be good enough: not for my father, not for school, not for my children, not for book critics, never quite enough. In some way, I never would come inside, a good position for a writer, but also, sometimes, a cold and fragile place.

For now, the little iPad and I limp on. I miss being high in the mountains. I miss all the rooms in the trees. And most of all, I miss standing on the edge of things, outside and cold and wild. And then, as now, I can also be inside, travelling, always travelling into adventure with a book, both reading and writing. I still have those. I read about mountain climbing, about sailing around Cape Horn in a clipper ship, about the first expedition to Antarctica. I read about animal languages and tree communication and mycelium and its mysterious adventures underground. I read whatever I can wrangle out of the library and the nearby bookstores. When I read, my heart stops jangling and my head goes quieter. So much to know, still. So happy to learn it, out here, on the edge of knowledge and understanding.

OLD MOTHER

My dog, Kinmont Willie, died in the middle of the afternoon. He collapsed on the floor and couldn't get up. He whined. His eyes begged me to help him. He had been aging slowly for a few years; he went deaf and was partially blind and because of this, he would never leave my side. When we went for walks, we walked slowly with his nose close to my hand, and still, occasionally, he fell over and was plainly bewildered by this failure of his body. He tried to jump a ditch one day, a shallow ditch over which he had jumped hundreds of times, and instead he fell, upside down, and lay there frightened. I had to kneel down and lift him, get his legs under him, and when he was up, he tried to gallop away to show me he was fine, that he hadn't actually fallen at all, but he almost fell again and so he stopped.

Eventually, he had a stroke and died.

I went to see my mother.

It was a thirty-minute drive to my mother's care home. A few years earlier, she'd had a stroke, and now she was banged up in a place she couldn't understand. Her short-term memory was gone, and although her long-term memories remained, she never really understood where she was. Or so I comforted myself. But she was always happy to see me.

As I drove, I rolled down the window and howled, howled for my dead dog and my lost mother and my painful poverty-sucking crippled writer's life, in which walks with my dog had been one of my biggest comforts.

When I came to the care home, my mother was sitting at a table in her wheelchair with a plate of blended mush in front of her. By now, she had lost the ability to feed herself. The care aides were rushed off their feet so it wasn't unusual to find her like this. I sat and fed her, one small plastic spoonful after another. She lifted her head like a bird and swallowed each spoonful, choking a bit on every one. I was simultaneously embarrassed and grateful. At first it had seemed so weird to spoon-feed my mother. Now I was grateful she was still there, and I could hold her hand and pat her back and have the same small conversation she and I have been having all my life.

"Would you like a cup of tea, Mom? And then we could go for a walk." I am not even sure she heard me. It didn't matter. All my life, I had come in her door, after school, after work, after anything, and she would put the kettle on and always there was tea and cookies, and just my mother being there.

We walked around the place, looked at the fish and then the turquoise and yellow plumed parakeets and the garden in which a few flowers still bloomed.

I howled for my dog when I got home as well, and then I went to find where my brother had buried him. I even lay on the ground for a while. It was immensely satisfying, to just let go and howl in grief and be melodramatic when there was no one to see or judge me.

The last time I had howled like that was not for when my father died of cancer, not for my mother in her wheelchair, but for my children when they left home. It started at the supermarket when I realized that I had no idea what to buy, no idea what I wanted to eat, that in fact there was almost nothing in the grocery store I wanted or needed, and I had no one else to feed. I bought a tin of salmon, and this time, back in the car, I howled all the way to the farm because missing my children was too much to bear. They had every right to leave and I had encouraged them to go. But somehow I hadn't realized that twenty years of cooking and cleaning meant that my life was now just mine, and it felt suddenly empty of everything that had given it meaning.

Eventually, I started to write a book to fill up the long silent evenings after work. The fridge door stayed closed. The stereo was silent. The television was silent. I had no idea what I wanted to watch or listen to, so I wrote a story for myself instead, a story where I was the lonely child hero, bereft of family, and finding my own way through the wild west.

When my children called, I told them I was fine, busy, working, writing, going for walks. And I was, after a very long while, okay with it all.

There's an odd phenomenon as you age, where you become, although still the mother, also someone to watch, someone who might, soon, become a problem. When my children were young, I watched them all the time, wondering who they would become, watched and judged and tried to help and got in the way and was annoying in every possible way but was still the mother, still had to be listened to.

And now I am the old mother, someone to be watched, judged, "looked after." Which is the last thing I want. When I have to die, I want to die alone, free of pity and care and sympathy.

I remember now, with shame, how much I ignored my mother, her failing memory, her fidgeting with her purse and shoes and jacket even to go out for a walk. How impatient I got, though I tried not to be. How I jollied her through cooking when she told me she couldn't remember recipes. We were so close but I still didn't understand what she was facing and how afraid she was, and now, too late, I do.

There are, in fact, many generation gaps, when parents and children misunderstand each other, many times when tempers flare on both sides. My generation invented that term; then it meant that our parents were particularly boring, hated rock music, had never tried drugs, couldn't run a computer, wore awful clothes. Now I am on the other side and completely unsure of the rules or what to say or do. Once my kids and I were ambitious together—we were working towards various goals and jobs and we achieved them. But then we got to live those lives we had achieved and we did. And now they don't need me, which is great. I finally have all my time to myself. But it doesn't stop me from worrying or missing them. That never goes away.

My generation were the boomers, the sixties kids, the revolutionaries, the change generators; we used the term "generation gap" proudly and derisively, and aimed it at our poor parents. We were the ones who first benefited from technology; in my life, I went from no phone to the phone on the wall with party lines and an operator, to my cherished cell phone and high-speed internet. As a writer, I am an information junkie. Way back in the dark ages, the beginning of this century, I finally got high-speed internet. My daughter, also a writer, and I would phone each other at midnight to see if we were both still trapped in the internet, clicking from site to site.

The fascination wore off pretty quickly and I went back to books. I had a brief flirtation with Kindle but it was too annoying to read. Books, more books. What is handy is that the internet is a good place to find books, read reviews, and find publishers, so I can get and read and write more books.

I wonder now how my mother and father felt about the changes they went through in their lifetimes. They were married in 1946. My father started farming with horses but quickly moved into farm machinery, which he kept running with a combination of ingenuity and cursing. They got a phone and a television but they never really gave either of these things a lot of attention. My father maintained a strong dislike of phoning long distance, which he was always convinced would cost a fortune, and the TV only went on at night, and then only to watch music or educational television.

But what did they think about their crazy children, their oldest daughter marching against the Vietnam war, and then marching for peace and the environment and feminism? We rarely talked about such things, so I still have no idea how much they comprehended of the work I did.

And drugs, the idea of which horrified them. Although as they got older, they bought more and more products at the health food store, and carefully tried out each new miracle pill or food or whatever came along.

But now I am finding myself on the other side of a different generation gap. My generation said, "Never trust anyone over thirty." But then we hit our thirties (some of us were amazed that we were still alive) and then our forties, which seemed pretty old, and then our fifties, when the idea of old started to gather speed, and now we are in our seventies and heading into our eighties, when we are genuinely old and, in my case, furious about it. As far as I am concerned, old age is the meanest trick my life has ever played on me, and I am so not ready for it. Will never be ready for it.

At the same time, I am finding myself in an odd relationship with my kids and grandkids. I am a social media junkie and proud of it, still writing, still working, still researching. But my kids and grandkids are now way ahead of me. I really don't have a clue what a bitcoin is or does, nor do I know or care about hashtags or Snapchat and a whole lot of other things. I have watched my grandkids grow up with the internet: Louis was eighteen months old when he shoved my hands off the keyboard and announced firmly, "Me do it" and ran off with the Teletubbies, who were clearly more fun than me.

I have very different goals now. Now I try to survive through each day with a minimum of pain and to stay alive long enough to read the gajillion books I still want to read plus write. Everything is still so interesting. I am still an information/reading/writing junkie. I am just so much slower. So although I write every day, I can't write at nearly the same speed I used to, nor can I work long into the night as I used to. Evenings are now for Netflix and the odd glass or two or three of wine.

My children's lives have settled into stasis too: working, kids, and mortgages, successful and great. What's to worry about?

Well, I'm still their mom. I worry about their health, their moods, their kids, their relationships. But I am no longer clear about what is expected of me from them, if anything. So how am I still a mother? I would still do anything for them but there is nothing to do. And what I feel saddest about is that they will go through what I am going through without me there to say, it's all right. It will be all right. It won't be. I will die and they will die after me. I find that thought unbearable.

My kids (and my friends—we watch each other) watch me in case I become that thing, that old parent who is a problem and needs fixing and care. I tiptoe a lot through conversational minefields, where I say, "I'm fine, I'm okay," all the time wondering, "Am I?"

I went to my fiftieth grad gathering, which I was basically blackmailed into (and which then turned out to be a lot of fun). But I was shocked and saddened when they read out the names of people who had died. I should not have been shocked, but I was and it surprised me. I now have a handshake familiarity with death, but as long as it stays outside of me, and I can keep working, I am mostly filled with a fierce joy that I am here, that the world is so beautiful, that my friends and children and grandchildren are so wonderful and interesting. Lots to do. Lots more still to learn. Not done yet.

And some days I carry my aging, recalcitrant, complaining, hurting body around with me like a burning stone I can't put down.

Somewhere, recently, I read that one of the harshest feelings of old age is feeling left behind. I don't feel left behind or irrelevant but sometimes I hear myself ranting and inside I am thinking, *Stop, Luanne, stop.* I watch the same old issues that we fought and fixed come around again and again, and some part of me watches astonished, dismayed, and amused, thinking, *We fought that. We won that fight.* Are humans somehow caught in an endless cycle of freedom, oppression, fighting the same issues over and over?

I have never believed this.

At the same time, I have no energy left to fight these battles again. It's not even a lack of energy so much as sheer puzzlement. I read history, I watch history, I want to know how it works.

I want to be prepared. I want to warn my grandkids. All these are futile desires. What am I supposed to do? How to act? What to say? Once I knew. I wrote a letter when I was eighteen to one of my university profs arrogantly chastising him for something I don't even remember. I don't remember what I said. I just remember saying it, full of clarity and certainty, certain I had discovered something that had been overlooked, or ignored. I carried that certainty for years.

And now, the greatest gift of aging is to be certain of nothing, to wake up every morning with one day to get through and no plans beyond that. The days go by fast. I write, I edit, I work on other people's work. Then I walk, I puff and pant up the hills while the dogs gallivant, noses to the ground. Princess Snowie, the white cat, still wafts her careful way just behind me. I look and I look. I try to perceive slow change. I have time for that now. I watch for significant events, the first dandelion, the first open leaves, the first swallow, frog, bat, osprey. The seasons turn so fast, but if I watch every day, I can catch parts and bit of the seasons as they turn and turn, even on grey winter days frozen fast to the ground, even on bright August days that I want to last forever.

And the nights when shadows flash and bump just at the edge of my vision, when I walk out just before bed to watch the stars jangle and dance, when the universe is so big and I am only a particle, and when death and I hold hands and smile at each other and go for a last walk before bed, then sometimes, just for a moment or two, it's all easy, it's all okay. Not howling, just dying slowly and okay with that.

THE PRICE OF SLOW

My cat insists on walking with me and the dogs when we go to the beach. If we don't go, she sits in the driveway with her back to me, sulking. Walking with a cat is a slow process. My cat has been attacked by eagles twice so she keeps a wary eye on the sky and will only walk across open spaces if I am right in front of her. And even then she stands, tail lashing, in a world full of danger. Where I live, for a white cat to have survived ten years of coyotes, owls, cougars, eagles, and other predators is remarkable but it makes for slow walking. She hides under brush, and then under the neighbour's porch. She stands and walks, stands and walks, hides, reappears. As soon as I am out of sight she howls, so I backtrack. Getting her to finally go somewhere is one process. Getting her to come home again through that labyrinth of danger is another; it involves a lot of calling, taking a few steps, calling, until she believes I am actually leaving and reluctantly, and equally slowly, follows me home.

On the way up from the lake one day, my beautiful white dog, Pearl, slows and lags. She lies down, gets up, stands with her nose to the ground. She looks at me, a deep look. She has dark eyes ringed with black hair. She stares at me. I stand over her, holding her head. It's okay, I say, it'll be okay. But she knows better. She is on her way somewhere I can't follow.

She hides on me that night, drags her dying body into the forest, under thick brush. I take a leash and will her home again, step by step. I pull her and she comes. She looks back at the forest. I tell her, no, you can die inside where it's warm.

The next morning, as soon as I let her out, she is gone again. I bring her in, phone the vet. My son comes and as he lifts her to put her in the car, she dies in his arms.

The price of slow is solitude and the price of slow is peace. The price of slow is the body and mind pulling away from each other, the mind zips on but the body won't follow. The price of slow is knees threatening to give way on my way up the stairs with two bags of groceries. Okay, put one back down, make two trips. The price of slow is no more gardening.

The gifts of slow are time to write, time to read, time to reflect. Slow is paradox, is ridiculousness, is contradiction, is time.

All my life was hurry, hurry hard. Early on the farm— hurry against the rain coming, get the hay in, get the cherries picked, get the weeds out of the garden, get the potatoes picked up, bring the cattle home. And in school, the joy and rush of reading books and then more books, so much to learn, to know, whole libraries to read. Faster, faster.

And the children coming, a house, an old truck, laundry, a few minutes writing alone in the bakery, with tea and a donut, luxury. Hurry home, hurry home. Things to do. Busy.

And then school in the city and working and kids and friends and books to write and university degrees and teaching and teaching. The mountain of things I carried every day, in those long, long days, a bag of notebooks and pens and a drawing book to doodle in, a laptop, a coffee mug, more books, essays to read and edit for students, and on the way home, rushing to the library for books and coming out with twenty, which then had to be carried, along with everything else up the hill in the rain before food or a meeting or an evening class and finally home and collapsing in front of some indistinguishable TV program. Just to stop, to sit in the dull purple light.

Oh, the rushing. The schedule. The daytimer with its scribbled notes and phone numbers and meetings and ideas and people to call and grants to write.

And the books, always the demands of books: books to write, books to read, books to edit, books for research. I have always slept with books sprayed across the covers, teetering on the bedside. Some nights they would all slide off, scuttle under the bed, try to leave me. But the dust balls corral them into place, they can never leave, despite the fines piling up at three libraries. And the ideas, sparkling and crackling through my brain at night. Write or sleep?

And then finally, moving back to the farm, and the new/old list of things to do again, gardens and flowers and trees to plant, trees to prune, rocks to wrestle into place, the dame of the demesne, that was me, and it was all good until it wasn't anymore.

Life slowed and slowed because things hurt, both mind and body. But I was trained from birth to cheat time: the rushing, the hurrying, the anxiety, the harvest, the huge dinners, the wine and the laughter and the friends. I missed it too much, the rushing and being just always over the edge of too busy and too much and too many and too fast, and my body said, done, done, and my mind said not yet, not yet.

But the body wins. Always wins, at some point. Even if the mind keeps crackling.

The peace of slow is walking slowly enough to catch, for the first time, slow change, to watch baby firs put out new tiny branches, to watch the first dandelion unfold, to watch for the night the leaves actually sift off the trees, to see the patterns of snow on rocks change every day. The reward of slow is mornings with coffee, books and Facebook friends— and long evenings with books and movies, the cat on my chest with her tiny snores, the dogs beside the bed, and dark coming in so slowly that I barely notice or care.

The body sets the boundaries but the mind is free, out of the cage of "busy" and "must" and "you should." Much as I hate aging, I acknowledge its gifts; the boundaries are those of energy but not of thought or imagination. But loss of energy is still a loss. Writing and thinking take more energy than I ever realized. And work is central to my sense of who I am.

My other work, essential for a writer, is walking and dreaming and looking at the world and everything in it to see what it has to tell me. Both of these kinds of work are intrinsically tied together and I can't do one without the other.

I still love working and I loved being a farmer, more than anything else I have done. People who aren't farmers (excluding the mechanized version of farming here) often say, "But farming is so much work." True, but it's far less work that spending eighty hours a week as a lawyer or a doctor, far less work than being stuck in a cubicle somewhere, and a whole lot more satisfying. The thing is farm work has to be done exactly when it needs to be, so even if the mosquitoes are howling in grey clouds, you go do hay or pick fruit. Even if it is belting down snow and wind, you feed and care for your animals before you go in. Even if your back is bent like an old pretzel, you hoe up the corn and hill up the potatoes.

But farm work was never hard work to me. My favourite thing to do when I was a kid was prune the apple trees. Once I got all the suckers and crossed branches out of the way, I could almost feel our old apple trees sighing and stretching and breathing. Of course, they just grew it all back again.

My father had two bad habits: he told us what to do but he never told us how, and no matter what we did or how hard we tried, it was never good enough. His biggest compliment to something we had done was to snort and walk away without criticism.

My dad also taught us to work until the job was finished; do not leave that bunch of cherries on the top branch of the tree or those few ripe ones hidden under the branches.

Farm life and farm work taught me many things: one was to work hard and one was to keep going. Farm work also taught me to wait and it taught me timing. Can't bring the hay in until it's dry. Can't milk the cow until it's milking time. Can't bake bread until it's risen.

And so, when it came to writing, I brought those lessons, plus the same level of intention and care to that work although "work" in writing is not always clear cut. Someone asked me once how I knew when a book was done. No book is ever completely done, but as Oscar Wilde says, once you're down to putting in commas and taking them back out, you are probably—maybe—done. Maybe.

The great thing about being a cultural worker is that you never have to retire. The arts will carry you through until the day you die. The great thing about writing and reading and editing is that when my heart decides we are staying home in the comfy chair for a bit, I can just keep on working.

I think a lot of people who are not artists don't quite realize that an artist, well, at least a writer, is always working. When I am writing a new something, I have to park it in the back of my brain and feed it rainbows and sparkles until I can get back to it, no matter what else I am doing. Otherwise, it will start to sulk and a sulky story is no fun to have around.

The worst advice someone can give me, is to "take it

easy." I don't know how and I don't want to learn. But now I am still learning, have had to learn to keep working within the boundaries that my body sets for me. I'm never going to make it to the top of a cherry tree again, but that keeps the robins and ravens happy.

I am practising slow change, which humans are bad at. The cat is teaching me. I am practising, when I can, to be in this place that I love as much as I can, as long as I can.

And more than anything now, I practise breathing, looking, thinking. Easy peasy.

Until it isn't.

ANOTHER COUNTRY

Somewhere a woman is grieving. Somewhere she is lying on a bed, almost asleep but not sleeping, feeling the night hours tick away with the rain; or somewhere this woman is walking, not far and not for long. All around her, tiny white flies form a thin mist. Grasshoppers spring from under her feet. A brown dragonfly hovers over a purple knapweed blossom. She studies the intricate tapestry at her feet. One day, she won't see these things anymore. They will stay and she will leave.

She is grieving but she is not sad. In fact, she watches as the new young dog, in the deep green heart of sunlit grass, gallops, leaps, puts his nose up, speeds in tight circles and comes back, drops to the ground where she stands, laughing at him. The dog's open red mouth pants with delight.

And tomorrow, she will drive her grandchildren to their music lessons, and buy them food and take them home.

Next week, she will have lunch with three of her closest friends, two of whom she will not see again, one surrendering slowly to illness, one moving away. She has been a loving woman in the world; she has many friends and children and grandchildren. But her friends are slowly leaving for other places, places with "access to healthcare," places without "mobility issues." They are clearing their houses, giving away art and books and dishes, favourite coffee cups, and clothes and their mother's china.

But that is not today. She has lived a long time within the beauty of the earth and she probes it for shadows, for faces that appear and vanish as she walks, for mystery, for clarity. She pauses often to look at the sky, the light, the water, the sweep of grass, always its own slow movie. She pauses to wait for the cat, which comes with her but sulks under bushes and watches the sky and beats at the boisterous dog with her claws.

The woman is very small and very large. She is very happy.

Grieving is not sad; it is just inevitable. Once she had all the world and all her plans and time to spend, and she spent it hard, working, and working more, and harder, and having dinners with friends and parties, and reading, always reading. Language the place she lived and still lives her other life, the words light up like beacons, always, no matter what else is happening.

Yet another evening, a dinner with a friend who is moving away. They have been close since high school, they raised their children together. It is unlikely they will meet again, too hard and too far to travel easily.

It is hard to know how to grieve or what exactly she is grieving. No one has died, not yet, although they are all on that long dark slide, holding on with doctors and medications and surgeries and careful daily walks and conversations with grandchildren.

Anything to hold on to, or with.

She doesn't know to hold this grief; everything continues, the syrupy taste of September grapes, the clouds clutching the mountain like beseeching children, the mountain burned orange from summer fires, but still valiant. What's a fire or two in a few million years?

All summer, smoke lay dense, dark iron grey, on the surface at the lake. At night, when the wind came, the smoke parted and the fire showed through. It was on the other side of the lake, but still huge. She could hear it. She stood on the deck in the wind, listening to the mountains burn. She loves these mountains. The trees will come back. Fire is natural. Things recover. But it was hard to watch, hard to pull herself away. The fire jumped, new fires steadily climbed all over the face of the mountain, new orange bursts exploded.

She knows about fire. She likes to burn things. Nothing better in the spring than to prune and rake and burn and tidy the world. She does it less and less. The world does not need her to clean it.

That's the thing—her life erodes, secretly, slowly. Not seeing people. Cutting back. Lying down. Walks are shorter, days are shorter. Writing is harder.

At night, the clutching of what? Fear, anxiety, depression? None of the words fit. A shifting into another country, the unknown, the place she wakes up to, the lack of balance, the slowness, life running down like a wound spring.

She hangs on, she hangs in, she walks, she cooks, she helps out, she comes home, her secret relief, a movie, wine and Tylenol, something good to read. Something interesting. Something informative. Something new. But why? Why the impatient flicking through so many bad movies? Why still search for knowledge through books on the climate crisis, forestry, mycelium, animal languages. Mysterious documentaries on quantum physics. What good is any of this knowledge?

That is what is leaving now, faster and faster. Purpose. The future. The things she will miss. High school graduations. University graduations. Long, loud family dinners.

And how it will all sort itself out—or not, that mysterious future, the one with climate change and more pandemics and food shortages and people fleeing floods and fires. The big question? Will humanity finally get it together or not? She really wants to know but instead, it drags on, all the bad sad news every morning that she reads with her coffee.

And she will not be here to take care of the grandchildren. They will have to find their own way. More than anything, she wants to be able to help them, explain how to survive, how she did whatever she had to do, how to keep going.

Outside, the jays swing from the sunflower seed heads, and the western conifer seed bugs, known everywhere as stinkbugs, sit on her keyboard and wave their teensy antennae with messages from the alien mothership, and the dogs lift their heads to see if she is tired of sitting around on such a beautiful morning and would much rather go out. Well, she would, but there are still deadlines and phone calls and work to be done.

Why can't she stop?

For the same reason her father said, as he was dying, "If I can't get out into the garden and do my work, why bother?" Well yes, that is the question.

There is still work to do and she does it, even though in the afternoons, pain comes in and she lies in bed, impatient, bored, waiting for it to recede, so she can get back up, write something, make food, whatever needs to be done. Keeping fed and clean takes a lot of time.

She wakes up every morning now to the raised faces and expectant tiny noises from the cats and the dogs, hanging out at the edge of the can opener. "Wait, wait," she murmurs, and they do, while she somehow simultaneously opens cans, spoons out food, makes coffee, tries to not get them mixed up, finally sinks into her chair, opens her computer to the dark splash of bad news, terrible news, reads and reads, finishes her coffee, then makes healthy food, oatmeal and applesauce, cleans, does dishes, carries out recycling, takes the laundry downstairs and chucks it in the machine, makes the bed despite the grumbles of the sleeping cat and finally sits back down again. Ready to begin.

Begin what? Another day in this other country, this mountain ridge of a day, trudging along it, balanced on that knife edge of *not falling*. Falling is painful. Causes shock. Breaks things.

This other country is made of new identities and new language. The new words seem to shape how she should live. She is supposed to "age gracefully," be somehow "sweet." She is an elder, a senior, aged, old. She is "mature" now, somewhat like an aged and rotting tree, or she is venerable, which is right on the edge of antique, which is right up there with obsolete.

The other gracefully aging people she meets know this language, but don't discuss it. They take care of themselves and each other. And when they query each other, "How are you?" they mean it with the emphasis on the *are*. Or they ask about the *thing*, how is it? Something broken, something cancerous, something not working. They are too familiar with waiting rooms and brisk, kindly nurses. When they meet, they discuss bad hospital food and then move on to other subjects.

Other people also ask, how are YOU!, meaning they have heard something, someone has said something to someone. What can she do but laugh, say, I'm good, I'm great. Things are great.

It is another country, a new country, a place where she is marginalized, teetering right on the edge of that insult, "She's doing so well for her age," or the worst one, "She's still so bright. Her memory is amazing." But not there yet.

Yes, her memory is amazing. That's because there is too damn much of it. Her brain is clogged with memories and sometimes they hurt. Her mother's face, always lifted with a smile when she came in the door. Her father's voice when he came in the basement to take off his boots and coveralls, play with the dog, come upstairs for dinner. The animals, the horses, the dogs, the kittens, loved and lost.

Somewhere in the September sun, the woman is both grieving and joyful, the universe shifts a little, time spins, the mountains will sprout green in the spring and perhaps she will watch for that and be glad.

Acknowledgements

I thank my brothers, Phil and Bill Armstrong, and my sister, Robin Armstrong. Particular thanks to Phil for his love and support, to Bill for his partnership at the farm, and to Robin for her gift of horses and riding, in particular, the gift of my horse, Caraigh.

To my brilliant and wonderful children, thanks for helping me grow and understand so much, for your amazing accomplishments, for your support when I needed you, and for my wonderful grandchildren. To those grandchildren, Tiger Lily, Tallullah, Elwood, Logan, Louis and Gaelin, thanks for your company and your many great questions.

To my adopted family, Ellie, Charles, Elijah, Celeste and Che Reynolds, your company and friendship has been a bright and joyful light in my life.

To my friends, fellow writers, and the warm and generous members of my writing groups, many thanks for hours of companionship, conversation, advice, ideas, discussion, thoughts and gatherings. I have been so gifted in my life with great teachers and mentors, and wonderful friends. I thank them all. Special deep gratitude for Jane Silcott and her incredible editing skills and ongoing support.

Deep thanks to Caitlin Press, Vici Johnstone, and Sarah Corsie for their support for this book and previous books.

And to my greatest teachers, the land, the water and their inhabitants, and to my many animal companions over the years, my deepest thanks of all.

About the Author

Luanne Armstrong holds a Ph.D in Education and an MFA in Creative Writing from the University of British Columbia. She has written twenty-five books, and has co-written or edited many other books through to publication. She has published novels, children's books, memoir and books of essays, as well as poetry. Her most recent books include a collection of poetry and photography titled *When We Are Broken: The Lake Elegy* (Maa Press), and the memoir *A Bright and Steady Flame* (Caitlin Press, 2018). She has won or been nominated for many awards, including the Chocolate Lily Award, the BC Hubert Evans Award, the Moonbeam Award, the Red Cedar Award, Surrey Schools Book of the Year Award, the Sheila A. Egoff Children's Literature Award, and the Silver Birch Award. Armstrong lives and works on the ancestral and unceded homelands of the Ktunaxa Nation and of the Sinixt People.